PEOPLE OF THE WORLD

By

Dee Phillips

Brian Alchorn, Catherine Chambers and David Dalton

ticktock

Copyright © **ticktock Entertainment Ltd 2006**

First published in Great Britain in 2006 by **ticktock Media Ltd.**,

Unit 2, Orchard Business Centre, North Farm Road, Tunbridge Wells, Kent, TN2 3XF

ISBN 1 86007 860 5 pbk

Printed in China

A CIP catalogue record for this book is available from the British Library.

We would like to thank: Steve Owen and Elizabeth Wiggans.

Picture credits t=top, b=bottom, c=centre, l=left, r=right
Alamy: 46t. Chernobyl Children's Project UK (Linda Walker): 38br. Corbis: 7b, 8tr 12b, 13bl, 18t, 18bl, 19t, 20, 26bl, 26br 30tr, 31c, 32b, 39t, 47b, 48t. Courtesy of Lost Boys of Sudan/www.LOSTBOYSFILM.COM: 9. Getty Images: 57t. Médecins Sans Frontieres: 28bl, 56t, 57b. Paul Jeffrey (Action by Churches Together): 8bl, 28tr. Superstock: 21t, 38t, 38bl, 40l, 46b, 47t, 51, 53. World Missionary Evangelism: 23. World Health Organisation: 29. World Image Library: 56.
Every effort has been made to trace the copyright holders, and we apologise in advance for any unintentional omissions. We would be pleased to insert the appropriate acknowledgements in any subsequent edition of this publication.
If the world were a village of 100 people... (page 7) courtesy of www.odt.org/pop.htm

CONTENTS

HOW TO USE THIS BOOK

JUST THE FACTS, PEOPLE OF THE WORLD is an easy-to-use, quick way to look up facts, research information about different cultures, and compare statistics on every country in the world. Each continent has its own section, and you will also find pages on migration, religions, celebrations and key issues. For fast access to *just the facts*, follow the tips on these pages.

BOX HEADINGS
Look for heading words linked to your research to guide you to the right fact box.

CONTINENT BY CONTINENT FACTS
Each continent's section opens with two pages that show key facts and statistics about the people of that continent.

TWO QUICK WAYS TO FIND A FACT:

1 Look at the detailed **CONTENTS** list on page 3 to find your topic of interest.

Turn to the relevant page and use the **BOX HEADINGS** to find the information box you need.

2 Turn to the **INDEX** which starts on page 61 and search for key words relating to your research.
• The index will direct you to the correct page, and where on the page to find the fact you need.

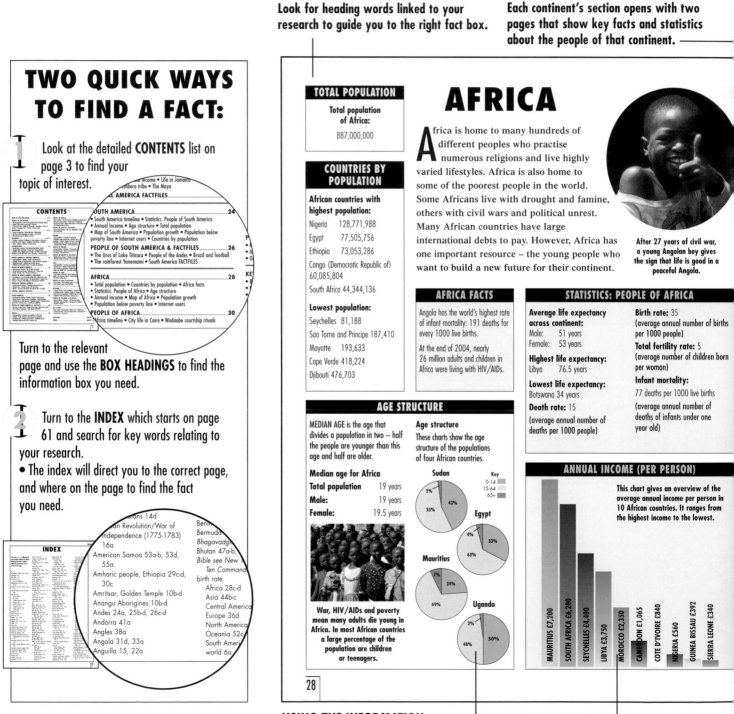

AFRICA

TOTAL POPULATION
Total population of Africa: 887,000,000

Africa is home to many hundreds of different peoples who practise numerous religions and live highly varied lifestyles. Africa is also home to some of the poorest people in the world. Some Africans live with drought and famine, others with civil wars and political unrest. Many African countries have large international debts to pay. However, Africa has one important resource – the young people who want to build a new future for their continent.

After 27 years of civil war, a young Angolan boy gives the sign that life is good in a peaceful Angola.

COUNTRIES BY POPULATION
African countries with highest population:
Nigeria 128,771,988
Egypt 77,505,756
Ethiopia 73,053,286
Congo (Democratic Republic of) 60,085,804
South Africa 44,344,136

Lowest population:
Seychelles 81,188
Sao Tome and Principe 187,410
Mayotte 193,633
Cape Verde 418,224
Djibouti 476,703

AFRICA FACTS
Angola has the world's highest rate of infant mortality: 191 deaths for every 1000 live births.
At the end of 2004, nearly 26 million adults and children in Africa were living with HIV/AIDs.

STATISTICS: PEOPLE OF AFRICA
Average life expectancy across continent:
Male: 51 years
Female: 53 years
Highest life expectancy: Libya 76.5 years
Lowest life expectancy: Botswana 34 years
Death rate: 15 (average annual number of deaths per 1000 people)

Birth rate: 35 (average annual number of births per 1000 people)
Total fertility rate: 5 (average number of children born per woman)
Infant mortality: 77 deaths per 1000 live births (average annual number of deaths of infants under one year old)

AGE STRUCTURE
MEDIAN AGE is the age that divides a population in two – half the people are younger than this age and half are older.
Median age for Africa
Total population 19 years
Male: 19 years
Female: 19.5 years

Age structure
These charts show the age structure of the populations of four African countries.

Sudan
Key
0-14
15-64
65+
2%
43%
55%

Egypt
4%
33%
63%

Mauritius
7%
24%
69%

Uganda
2%
48%
50%

War, HIV/AIDs and poverty mean many adults die young in Africa. In most African countries a large percentage of the population are children or teenagers.

ANNUAL INCOME (PER PERSON)
This chart gives an overview of the average annual income per person in 10 African countries. It ranges from the highest income to the lowest.

MAURITIUS £7,200
SOUTH AFRICA £6,200
SEYCHELLES £4,400
LIBYA £3,750
MOROCCO £2,350
CAMEROON £1,065
COTE D'IVOIRE £840
NIGERIA £560
GUINEA BISSAU £392
SIERRA LEONE £340

USING THE INFORMATION
Facts and statistics can be compared between different countries and different continents to build up a picture of the differences and similarities between regions.

JUST THE FACTS
Each topic box presents the facts you need in lists; short, quick-to-read bullet points; charts and tables.

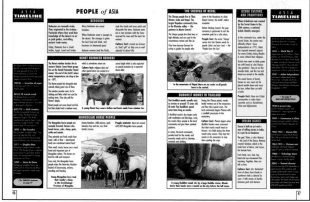

The chapter for each continent has a history timeline and boxes supplying information about different cultures and lifestyles

The chapter for each continent includes FACTFILES for every country giving facts and statistics in many categories.

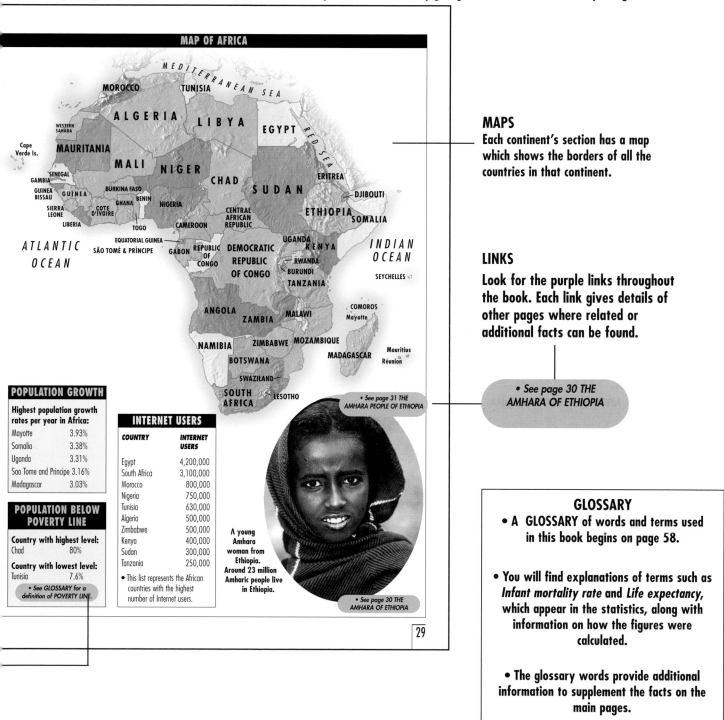

MAP OF AFRICA

MAPS

Each continent's section has a map which shows the borders of all the countries in that continent.

LINKS

Look for the purple links throughout the book. Each link gives details of other pages where related or additional facts can be found.

• See page 30 THE AMHARA OF ETHIOPIA

• See page 31 THE AMHARA PEOPLE OF ETHIOPIA

A young Amhara woman from Ethiopia. Around 23 million Amharic people live in Ethiopia.

• See page 30 THE AMHARA OF ETHIOPIA

POPULATION GROWTH

Highest population growth rates per year in Africa:

Mayotte	3.93%
Somalia	3.38%
Uganda	3.31%
Sao Tome and Principe	3.16%
Madagascar	3.03%

INTERNET USERS

COUNTRY	INTERNET USERS
Egypt	4,200,000
South Africa	3,100,000
Morocco	800,000
Nigeria	750,000
Tunisia	630,000
Algeria	500,000
Zimbabwe	500,000
Kenya	400,000
Sudan	300,000
Tanzania	250,000

• This list represents the African countries with the highest number of Internet users.

POPULATION BELOW POVERTY LINE

Country with highest level:
Chad   80%

Country with lowest level:
Tunisia   7.6%

• See GLOSSARY for a definition of POVERTY LINE.

GLOSSARY

• A GLOSSARY of words and terms used in this book begins on page 58.

• You will find explanations of terms such as *Infant mortality rate* and *Life expectancy*, which appear in the statistics, along with information on how the figures were calculated.

• The glossary words provide additional information to supplement the facts on the main pages.

WORLD POPULATION

In the past 200 years the world's population has grown and grown:

1820	1 billion
1930	2 billion
1960	3 billion
1974	4 billion
1988	5 billion
2000	6 billion

Total world population 2005:
6,446,131,400

Highest population:
China 1,306,313,812

World population growth per year:
1.14%

BIRTH AND DEATH STATISTICS TOTAL WORLD POPULATION

Life expectancy at birth:
Male: 63 years
Female: 66 years

Highest life expectancy:
Andorra, Europe 83.5 years

Lowest life expectancy:
Botswana, Africa 34 years

Death rate: 9
(average annual number of deaths per 1000 people)

Birth rate: 20
(average annual number of births per 1000 people)

Total fertility rate: 2.6
(number of children born per woman)

Infant mortality:
50 deaths per 1000 live births
(average annual number of deaths of infants under one year old)

Today billions of people from thousands of different ethnic groups and many, many countries will go to work, eat and drink, practise their religions and customs, and enjoy celebrations. Wars will be fought, and people will die. Babies will be born and families will rejoice. For the hundreds of ways in which we are all different, there are hundreds of ways in which we are all the same. We number over 6 billion – we are the *people of the world*.

PEOPLE OF THE WORLD BY AGE GROUP

27.8% of the world's population is aged 0 to 14 years.

64.9% of the world's population is aged 15 to 64 years.

7.3% of the world's population is aged 65 years and over.

PEOPLE OF THE WORLD – FAST FACTS

North America
Every year, 1 million immigrants from around the world begin new lives in the USA.

Every year, a huge marathon race is run in New York. In 2004, more than 35,000 runners, from around the world, finished the 26.2-mile race.

South America
More than 50 per cent of South America's population lives in just one country, Brazil.

Africa
Around 3000 different ethnic groups have been identified in Africa. People from a particular ethnic group are often found in several different countries.

It is not usual in African cultures to write down historical and cultural information, it is passed from person to person through art, songs and by spiritual leaders.

Europe
Christianity has been the main religion in Europe since the days of the Roman Empire, 2000 years ago.

Europe has produced many world famous artists, such as Picasso and Van Gogh, famous writers, such as Shakespeare, and famous composers, such as Beethoven and Mozart.

Asia
Many central Asian peoples live nomadic lives, so their art forms, such as music, jewellery and textiles, are portable. Beautiful hand-woven rugs often represent a family's *'savings'*, just as money or jewellery does in other parts of the world.

All the world's major religions started on the continent of Asia.

Oceania
Very few people live in the Australian *'outback'* – the vast, dry, central part of Australia. Over 80% of Australia's population live in cities and towns on the coast.

IF THE WORLD WERE A VILLAGE OF 100 PEOPLE...

It can be very difficult to fully grasp the huge numbers involved when talking about the world's population. The *'State of the Village Report'* was first compiled in the 1990s to give a unique overview of the world's people. Data is collected from many sources and the report is regularly updated.

IF THE WORLD WERE A VILLAGE OF ONLY 100 PEOPLE THERE WOULD BE:

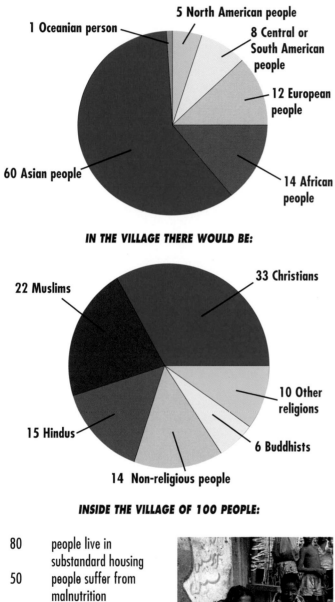

- 5 North American people
- 8 Central or South American people
- 12 European people
- 14 African people
- 60 Asian people
- 1 Oceanian person

IN THE VILLAGE THERE WOULD BE:

- 33 Christians
- 10 Other religions
- 6 Buddhists
- 14 Non-religious people
- 15 Hindus
- 22 Muslims

INSIDE THE VILLAGE OF 100 PEOPLE:

80	people live in substandard housing
50	people suffer from malnutrition
33	people have no access to safe drinking water
24	people do not have any electricity
7	people own a car

In the village there are 42 radios, 24 televisions, 14 telephones and 7 computers.

Children living in a Calcutta slum, in India, scrounge for food in a pile of rubbish.

LANGUAGES

Nearly 7000 different languages are spoken around the world today.

NUMBERS OF SPEAKERS

The table below shows the number of speakers of the world's 10 major languages. The figures apply to people who speak the language as their first language (many people speak more than one language).

LANGUAGE	NUMBER OF SPEAKERS	%WORLD POPULATION
• Chinese (Mandarin)	881 million	13.69%
• Spanish	325.5 million	5.05%
• English	312 million	4.84%
• Hindi	181.7 million	2.82%
• Portuguese	178.5 million	2.77%
• Bengali	172.7 million	2.68%
• Russian	146 million	2.27%
• Japanese	128 million	1.99%
• German (Standard)	96 million	1.49%
• Chinese (Wu)	78 million	1.21%

(Figures calculated from the CIA world factbook 2004 estimates.)

LANGUAGE FACTS

- Just over half of the world's languages are spoken by fewer than 10,000 people.

- Only around 350 languages have over 1 million users.

- English is the language that has the widest geographical distribution.

- In both Africa and Asia over 2000 different languages are spoken.

- South America is sometimes called *Latin America* because most people speak Spanish and Portuguese, which are Latin-based languages.

- While the population of Papua New Guinea is just 5.5 million, between them the people speak over 800 different languages!

LITERACY

The percentage of the world's population aged 15 and over who can read and write:

Total population: 77%

Male: 83%

Female: 71%

INTERNET USERS

Number of people using the Internet worldwide: 604,111,719

Some people may use the Internet every day, others may only have access to a computer once or twice a year.

MIGRATION

Since humans first walked out of Africa 100,000 years ago, people have been on the move. When large numbers of people move, and then stay put, we say they have migrated. Today, because of migration, most countries around the world are a mix of different ethnic groups and cultures. This can cause tension, but most people live together in mutual tolerance. There is likely to be more migration in the future, so more of us are going to live in diverse, multi-cultural societies.

CAUSES OF MIGRATION

- **Pushes** make people leave where they are because they are poor, hungry, frightened or in danger.

- **Pulls** make people go to a particular destination because they hope to find land, work, food, safety or freedom there.

URBANISATION: COUNTRY LIFE TO TOWNS

One of the earliest examples of urbanisation was during the Industrial Revolution in the 18th and 19th centuries. In Britain, large numbers of people moved from the countryside to find factory jobs in the new industrial cities.

Nowadays, urbanisation is happening fastest in the poor countries of the world. City populations are growing at up to 12% a year as people move to cities hoping to find jobs.

- Bangkok, Thailand, grew from 2 million people to 7 million between 1960 and 1990.

- Mexico City (the capital of Mexico) grew by 5 million people between 1985 and 1995.

- Between 1990 and 1995 the cities of the developing world grew by 263 million people.

c1900 – European immigrants who have passed through the entry station at Ellis Island, New York, USA, wait for the ferry that will transport them to New York City to begin their new lives in America.

NATURAL DISASTERS

Earthquakes, volcanic eruptions, floods and droughts can kill and injure thousands of people. Thousands more may be displaced for a short time, but they soon return home. Why?

- Volcanic soils and flood-plains are fertile.
- Earthquakes are infrequent and unpredictable.

- Droughts, while frequent in many African countries, are not usually a good enough reason for people to leave their homes permanently. However, in 2004, the government of Ethiopia announced a plan to move 2 million people from the drought-prone highlands to more fertile areas with better rainfall.

Ethiopian families walk back to their village after collecting food aid during a drought in the northern highlands of Ethiopia.

THE SLAVE TRADE

- Between 1648 and 1815, slave traders took up to 9 million people from West Africa to be slaves in North America, South America and the Caribbean islands (Central America).

- This is the reason that black people make up the majority of the population on many Caribbean islands, and large minorities in the USA and Brazil.

- A similar slave trade operated in east Africa, where up to a million people were taken to countries in the Middle East during the same period of time as the Atlantic trade.

MIGRATIONS IN THE USA

- During the first half of the 20th century, black people moved from the southern states of the USA, where their forefathers had been slaves, to the cities of the North and California.

- In the second half of the 20th century, Spanish-speaking immigrants from Mexico and Central America came to the USA looking for a better life. There are now 37 million Hispanics in the USA.

NEW WORLDS

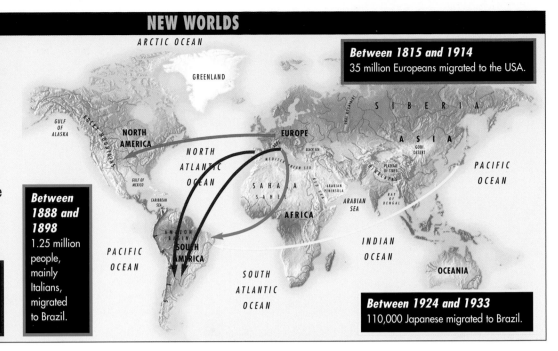

From the 18th century onwards, millions of Europeans migrated to North and South America, Australia and New Zealand, and parts of Africa.

Some were pushed by poverty. Some by persecution. Others were pulled by land, opportunity and freedom.

Between 1857 and 1930
3.5 million people, mainly Italians and Spaniards, migrated to Argentina.

Between 1888 and 1898
1.25 million people, mainly Italians, migrated to Brazil.

Between 1815 and 1914
35 million Europeans migrated to the USA.

Between 1924 and 1933
110,000 Japanese migrated to Brazil.

WAR AND PERSECUTION

Wars force people to flee for their lives. As soon as the war is over, most of them return home. People who are persecuted for their religion, opinions, or race, may flee and not return.

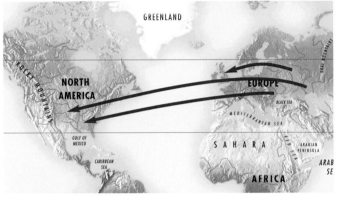

Between 1900 and 1914
Over 1.5 million Jews migrated to the USA to escape persecution in Russia and eastern Europe. Many others fled to Britain.

1947 – Independence in India and Pakistan
When India gained independence from Britain in 1947, it was divided into Muslim Pakistan and Hindu India. Hindus did not want to be a minority in Muslim Pakistan, and Muslims did not want to be a minority in Hindu India. Over 17 million people migrated between the two countries.

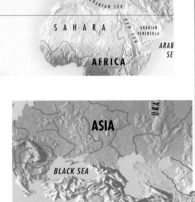

In 2001, nearly 4000 young men and teenage boys migrated from Sudan, in Africa to the USA. They were seeking peace, freedom and education. The boys had spent their childhoods in refugee camps during Sudan's 21-year civil war.

• 7.5 million Muslims migrated from India to West Pakistan.

• 1 million Muslims left India for East Pakistan (now Bangladesh).

• 5.5 million Hindus migrated from West Pakistan to India.

• 3.3 million Hindus left East Pakistan (now Bangladesh) for India.

MOTHER COUNTRIES

During the 1950s and 1960s, people from the colonies and ex-colonies of European countries migrated to their 'mother countries' in search of a better life.

• Black people from the Caribbean, and Asians from India, Pakistan and Bangladesh (previously East Pakistan) migrated to Britain.

• In France, many migrants are Muslims from North Africa.

• Germany did not have colonies, but people from southern Europe, and especially Turkey, moved to find work in German cities. Between 1955 and 1973, 5.1 million migrants worked in Germany.

• See page 39
MULTI-CULTURAL LONDON
and
MUSLIM COMMUNITY OF PARIS.

• See pages 41 to 43
EUROPE FACTFILES to research the ethnic mix of FRANCE, GERMANY and the UNITED KINGDOM

RELIGION TIMELINE

2000-1500 BCE — Judaism
Prophets Abraham, Isaac, Jacob, Joseph and Moses bring together the beliefs and practices of Judaism, including the *Ten Commandments* (a list of religious rules).

• See the GLOSSARY for explanations of BCE/CE

1200 BCE — Vedas
The Hindu religion's *'Vedas'* are composed. Vedas are scriptures, hymns and verses written in Sanskrit (an ancient Indian language).

660 BCE — Shinto religion
The Japanese Shinto religion develops. It honours nature spirits.

6th century BCE
Zoroaster founds Zoroastrianism in Persia. Lao-tzu founds Taoism in China. Tao means *'the path'* and stresses the importance of unity and harmony.

599-527 BCE — Jainism
Mahavira, an Indian chieftain's son, founds Jainism in India. Jains harm no living thing.

551-479 BCE — Confucianism
Chinese philosopher Confucius (or Kongzi) founds Confucianism in China. It is a guide to how we should behave and treat each other.

528 BCE — Buddhism
Prince Siddharta Gautama (Buddha) founds Buddhism in India.

• See page 13 BUDDHA'S BIRTH, ENLIGHTENMENT AND DEATH

c200 BCE — Bhagavadgita
The Hindu *'Bhagavadgita'* is composed by an unknown poet. It is 700 verses on Hinduism.

CE 50-150 — New Testament
The Christian New Testament is put together in Palestine. It includes the teachings of Jesus Christ as heard by his closest followers, the Apostles.

610-622 — Holy Qu'ran
The Holy Qu'ran is revealed to the Holy Prophet Muhammad. Islam begins in Medina (now in modern-day Saudi Arabia).

• The TIMELINE continues on page 11.

Religion is the belief in a power or powers beyond our understanding. Belief systems, or religions, try to explain how the world was created, why we are here and what happens when we die. They try to establish social order, too. Some religions are quite local, with few followers; others are global, with millions. Today, many religions combine ancient traditions with newer belief systems.

A Hindu *sadhu* (holy man). Sadhus give up worldly possessions and devote their lives to praying and teaching.

NUMBERS OF FOLLOWERS OF MAJOR RELIGIONS

This table shows the numbers of people following the world's major religions.

The table also shows the numbers of people who are non-religious (they do not belong to any specific faith) and those who are atheist — they do not believe that god exists.

(Figures calculated from the CIA world factbook)

- Jews 0.23%
- Sikhs 0.39%
- Muslims 19.9%
- Other religions 12.63%
- Non-religious 12.44%
- Atheists 2.36%
- Buddhists 5.92%
- Hindus 13.29%
- Christians 32.84%

HOLY PLACES AROUND THE WORLD

1) GOLDEN TEMPLE, AMRITSAR
Place of Sikh pilgrimage. The gold-covered temple stands in the middle of a pool – *The Pool of Nectar*. A magnificent copy of the sacred text, the *Guru Granth Sahib*, is inside.

2) JERUSALEM
Jews, Christians and Muslims make pilgrimages to holy sites in Jerusalem. Jews: the *Wailing Wall* – the only remains of the Second Temple of Jerusalem destroyed by the Romans in CE 70. Christians: the *Church of the Holy Sepulchre* – the site of Jesus Christ's crucifixion. Muslims: *the Dome of the Rock* – a shrine believed to be the site from which Muhammad ascended to heaven.

3) KANDY, SRI LANKA
A Buddhist pilgrimage site. Here the *Temple of the Tooth* houses the Buddha's tooth.

4) MECCA AND MEDINA
At Mecca the Great Mosque and the holy *Kaaba* shrine (a large, cube-shaped, granite building) are the

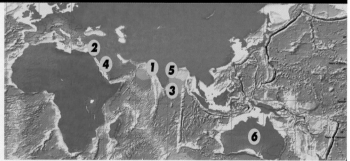

central point of Muslim pilgrimages, or Hajj.

• See the GLOSSARY for information about HAJJ.

5) VARANASI
Place of pilgrimage for Hindus. At Varanasi, Hindus bathe in the sacred waters of the River Ganges. Some Hindus have their ashes scattered on the river when they die.

6) ULURU, CENTRAL AUSTRALIA
The giant, red rock Uluru is a sacred site for Australian

Aborigines, dating back to the dawn of the world, *'dreamtime'*. The religious artworks in its caves are thousands of years old, but the paint is continually renewed.

• See page 54 ABORIGINES AND DREAMTIME

The Anangu Aborigines have lived near Uluru for around 20,000 years.

HINDUISM

- **Followers:** Hindus
- **Beliefs:** *Brahman* is the creator and foundation of everything – many other Hindu gods stem from Brahman. *Samsara* is the cycle of birth and rebirth. *Karma* is the belief that how we act affects our next life.
- **Duties:** Goodness and prayer, called *puja*.
- **Texts:** The *Vedas* which are scriptures revealed by a spiritual source.

Hindu pilgrims bathe in the River Ganges at Varanasi, India.

ISLAM

- **Followers:** Muslims – mainly Sunni, Shi'a and Sufi groupings.
- **Beliefs:** Allah, the one God, and Muhammad as his Prophet.
- **Duties:** *The Five Pillars of Islam:* declaration of faith, praying 5 times a day, giving charity, fasting and pilgrimage to Mecca.
- **Texts:** The *Holy Qu'ran* (Muslim scriptures as revealed to the Holy Prophet Muhammad).

BAHA'I

- **Followers:** Baha/Baha'is.
- **Beliefs:** Harmony, equality and the unification of all religions.
- **Duties:** Faith in Baha'u'llah, prayer and fasting.
- **Texts:** The *Kitab-al-Aqdas, The Most Holy Book'* (containing Baha'u'llah's laws and moral truths). *Kitab-e-Iqan, The Book of Certitude* (teachings on religions and the nature of God).

SIKHISM

- **Followers:** Sikhs
- **Beliefs:** One god, who is the Truth.
- **Duties:** Seeking Truth, goodness, hard work and prayer.
- **Texts:** The *Guru Granth Sahib* (a sacred book of teachings, it is *the Word*).

BUDDHISM

- **Followers:** Buddhists
- **Beliefs:** Enlightenment achieved through good thoughts, acts and words.
- **Duties:** To follow the *Four Noble truths* and the *Eightfold Path* to enlightenment.

> • See the GLOSSARY for the FOUR NOBLE TRUTHS and the EIGHTFOLD PATH

Texts: The *Tripitaka* (the rules for monks; the original teachings of the Buddha; the deep meaning of Buddhism).

JUDAISM

- **Followers:** Jews – mainly Conservative, Orthodox (traditional) and Reform groupings.
- **Beliefs:** There is only one God.
- **Duties:** to follow the *Ten Commandments* given to Moses by God, and the *Torah*.
- Texts: The *Tanakh* or Hebrew bible, the *Torah* (teachings) and the *Talmud* (Jewish laws or how to live).

ZOROASTRIANISM

- **Followers:** Zoroastrians or Parsis (in India).
- **Beliefs:** Good creator god, Ahura Mazda, and negative force, Ahriman. Good will overcome evil.
- **Duties:** Good thoughts, good words, good deeds
- **Texts:** The *Avesta* (a sacred book of laws, teachings and hymns, called *gathas*).

CHRISTIANITY

- **Followers:** Christians of many denominations, for example, Roman Catholics and Protestants.
- **Beliefs:** God – as the Father, the Son (Jesus Christ), and the Holy Spirit.
- **Duties:** Love, compassion, prayer and worship.
- **Texts:** *New Testament* (the life, teachings and parables of Christ. Also the beginnings of the spread of the Christian Church after his crucifixion).

The Soweto gospel choir from South Africa. Christian gospel music is a passionate, highly rhythmic way of singing religious songs.

RELIGION TIMELINE

632 – The first Caliph
The Holy Prophet Muhammad dies in 632. Islam continues through the first Caliph (Muslim spiritual leader) Abu Bakr, who was one of Muhammad's first followers.

> • See page 13
> EID UL FITR AND RAMADAN (MUSLIM FESTIVAL)

1054 – Christian split
Christianity splits into the western Church of Rome (Roman Catholic) and the eastern Church of Constantinople (Orthodox). It is known as the 'schism', the split was the end result of many disagreements.

1500s – Sikhism
Sikhism is founded by Sri Guru Nanak in Punjab, India.

> • See page 12
> VAISAKHI (SIKH FESTIVAL)

1517 – Martin Luther
In Germany, priest Martin Luther believes that the Catholic Church has become corrupt. He issues a list of 95 statements attacking the church, then denies the authority of the Pope (the head of the Catholic Church). It is the beginning of the *Reformation* (changes in church practice) and Protestantism – the Christian Church without a pope.

1604 – Sikh holy texts
The tenth Sikh Guru (spiritual leader) decrees that after his death, Sikhs should in future follow the teachings in the *Guru Granth Sahib*. The texts become the final Sikh Guru in 1604.

1863 – Baha'i faith
The Baha'i faith is founded by Baha'u'llah in Tehran, Persia (modern-day Iran).

1930s – Rastafarianism
Rastafarianism is founded in Jamaica. It is inspired by the political activist Marcus Garvey who wants African Americans to return to their African roots. Rastafarians believe that Emperor Haile Selassie the First of Ethiopia (known as *Ras Tafari*) is *Jah* (God).

SPECIAL DAYS & FESTIVALS

Carnival

Every spring in the days leading up to Ash Wednesday (in the Christian calendar) thousands of people celebrate carnival on the streets of Rio de Janeiro, in Brazil. They dance, they sing and they wear fabulous costumes. In Venice, Italy, masked balls and parades take place to celebrate *carnevale*.

Chinese New Year

This festival begins on the first day of the lunar calendar, often in February. Celebrations last for many days. Bad spirits are swept out, lucky red slogans are painted on doors and lucky red parcels of money are given. A new 'Animal of the Year' begins its reign.

Christian Saints' Days

There are hundreds of Saints' days throughout the year. Every May, in St Maries de la Mer, France, European Romanies gather to honour their patron saint, Sara. Her statue is paraded then dipped into the sea.

• See page 39 THE ROMA.

Christmas Eve

In the Christian calendar Christmas Day (Jesus Christ's birthday) is always on the 25 December. Christmas Eve is therefore the 24 December. In Melbourne, Australia, 40,000 people sing carols (Christmas hymns) at the Sidney Myer Music Bowl. In the Vatican City 10,000 worshippers attend Midnight Mass.

Eid ul Adha

This moveable Muslim feast takes place during the twelfth Muslim month. It marks the end of Hajj, which is the pilgrimage to Mecca, and when Allah asked the Prophet Abraham to sacrifice his son, Isaac. A goat is slaughtered and its meat is given to the poor.

• See THE GLOSSARY for more information about words and terms, such as HAJJ, used in this section.

People celebrate all over the world to mark important events. Some celebrations are personal, while others are religious, seasonal or political. Many help us to remember the lives of good people. The dates of some celebrations are the same every year. Others are moveable – changing because they follow the lunar calendar. Feasting, fasting, dancing and praying are all ways of marking these special times.

At *Thanksgiving*, celebrated in the USA, a special meal of turkey, cranberry sauce and pumpkin pie is enjoyed.

BAR MITZVAH/BAT MITZVAH (JEWISH)

At his Bar Mitzvah a 13-year-old boy becomes *a son of the commandment*. A 12-year-old girl becomes *a daughter of the commandment* at her bat mitzvah.

Originally only for boys, but now a time for both boys and girls to accept responsibility for their own actions. At traditional synagogues, boys read the *Torah* for the first time in front of others in the synagogue. In progressive synagogues, both girls and boys can read from the Torah.

The boys' ceremony began in the Middle Ages — the girls, only began in the 20th century.

Parties are held to celebrate the occasion and gifts are given to the boy or girl.

A boy reads from the *Torah,* in a synagogue, during his Bar Mitzvah His parents and rabbi (religious leader) are closeby.

EASTER FOOD

During this Christian festival, people in Greece eat spring lamb and bread with dyed, hard-boiled eggs sunk into it. In Russia, a dessert called pashka is enjoyed. Pashka is made from soft cheese, cream, orange peel and dried fruit.

VAISAKHI (SIKH AND HINDU)

This Sikh and Hindu festival is celebrated all over the world.

Vaisakhi is celebrated in April. In ancient times Vaisakhi marked the end of the spring harvest in the Punjab, in India.

At this time, Sikhs also celebrate Guru Gobhind Singh's creation of the *Khalsa*. Meaning 'pure', the Khalsa is a group of Sikh elders who defend the Sikh faith.

People attend the *Gurdwara* (temple) and a great meal is prepared in the Gurdwara's *langar* (the temple kitchen). Sharing food is very important to Sikhs. Processions also take place through the streets.

Sikh Khalsa members wear five important symbols: uncut hair, a hair-comb, a sword, short trousers and a steel unity bracelet.

DEEPAVALI FOOD

At Deepavali, Hindus and Sikhs eat sweets such as halva, made from semolina and pistachio nuts perfumed with rose water and cardamon.

BUDDHA'S BIRTH, ENLIGHTENMENT & DEATH

This celebration has different names in different Buddhist cultures — *Buddha Jayanti* in India and Nepal; *Saka Dawa* in Tibet.

Buddha's birth, enlightenment and death occurred on the same date — the 15th day of the fourth month in the Buddhist calendar — but in different years.

It is celebrated in different ways all over the Buddhist world.

In Tibet, people light yak-butter lamps in the temples, and the Jokhang Temple in Lhasa city is packed with worshippers.

A statue of Buddha, at a Buddhist temple in Japan. Buddhist temples vary in their design from country to country, but they all have a statue of the Buddha.

EID UL FITR AND RAMADAN (MUSLIM)

Eid ul Fitr is a celebration held at the end of the month of Ramadan, the ninth month in the Muslim lunar calendar.

Eid ul Fitr celebrates the end of the month-long fast of Ramadan when Muslims do not eat or drink from dawn until dusk. Eid ul Fitr begins when a sliver of the new moon is spied in the sky.

Ramadan honours the time when the Holy Prophet Muhammad received the *Word of God* in a harsh mountain cave.

During the fast, Muslims think about people who have little food to eat and money is given to the poor.

Muslims break the fast with dates and milk. There is festive food and children wear new clothes, eat sweets and are often given spending money.

Indian Muslims attend morning Eid prayer during the holy month of Ramadan at the Jama Masjid mosque in Old Delhi, India.

EID UL ADHA FOOD

During this Muslim festival meals of goat meat, spiced rice, dates, fruit and sweets are enjoyed.

EASTER (CHRISTIAN)

Easter is the most important Christian celebration of the year. It marks the death of Jesus Christ (Good Friday) and his resurrection three days later (Easter Sunday).

Easter takes place after the 40-day Lent period — a time of fasting. Easter is a moveable feast which falls in March or April each year.

Christians in much of Europe and South and Central America hold candlelit vigils in church on *Holy Saturday* or *Easter Eve*. At midnight, the church is flooded with light and flowers as people proclaim, "Christ is Risen".

Some Easter traditions, such as the giving of decorated eggs, date back to pre-Christian spring festivals.

Easter eggs

CHRISTMAS FOOD

In Portugal, people eat *bolacha do Rei* (cake of the King) — a round cake with a central hole and glacé fruits. In the Czech Republic carp fish is enjoyed, and in Spain and Italy, nutty nougats are a Christmas treat.

SPECIAL DAYS & FESTIVALS

Argungu fishing festival
This exciting event takes place in northern Nigeria. Thousands of fisherman run into the water with fishing nets. After one hour, the man with the largest fish wins!

Halloween
This ancient pre-Christian ceremony is always held on 31 October. Many hundreds of years ago, people believed it was when the spirits of the dead returned. Bonfires were lit to ward off evil spirits and people wore masks to hide themselves from evil ghosts. Today children wear scary costumes to go door to door *Trick or Treating*!

Hannukah
Celebrated in the Jewish month of Kislev (December). This eight-day *Jewish Festival of Light*, celebrates the great victory of Jews against the Syrians in 165 BC. Candles are lit each night to remember recapturing the Temple in Jerusalem following the victory.

Holi
This Hindu festival welcomes the spring. It is particularly celebrated in the north of India. The night before Holi, bonfires are lit to show the destruction of Holika, the evil demon. Next day, everyone throws brightly-coloured powder and dye over each other.

Pongal
Tamil people in India celebrate *Pongal* in mid-January. It is a four-day celebration of the end of harvest. Huge pots of pongal (rice, dahl, sugar and milk) are made to boil over — this symbolises good harvest and wealth.

Thanksgiving
Thanksgiving is held in the USA every year on the fourth Thursday in November. It celebrates the *Pilgrim Fathers'* good harvest of 1621. Families return home from far and wide to celebrate. There are Thanksgiving parades and American football games.

> • See THE GLOSSARY for more information about words and terms, such as TRICK OR TREATING, used in this section.

TOTAL POPULATION

Total population of North America:
328,600,000

Total population of Central America:
185,800,000

This little girl is just one of the 40% of Mexicans who live below the poverty line.

NORTH AMERICA
& CENTRAL AMERICA

The continents of North and Central America have been settled by people from so many parts of the world that they are sometimes called the *'melting pot'*. More cultures and religions are intermingled in this region than anywhere else on Earth. The people also live in a varied range of environments from frozen areas in the north, such as Greenland and Alaska, to the deserts of Mexico and the rainforests of Costa Rica in the south.

A young Cherokee man dresses in traditional costume at a *pow-wow*, a gathering of American Indian tribes.

STATISTICS: PEOPLE OF NORTH AMERICA

Average life expectancy across continent:
Male: 73.5 years
Female: 80 years

Highest life expectancy:
Canada 80 years

Lowest life expectancy:
Greenland 70 years

Death rate: 7.5
(average annual number of deaths per 1000 people)

Birth rate: 14
(average annual number of births per 1000 people)

Total fertility rate: 2
(number of children born per woman)

Infant mortality:
9 deaths per 1000 live births
(average annual number of deaths of infants under one year old)

STATISTICS: PEOPLE OF CENTRAL AMERICA

Average life expectancy across continent:
Male: 70.5 years
Female: 75 years

Highest life expectancy:
Cayman Islands 80 years

Lowest life expectancy:
Haiti 53 years

Death rate: 7
(average annual number of deaths per 1000 people)

Birth rate: 19
(average annual number of births per 1000 people)

Total fertility rate: 2.5
(number of children born per woman)

Infant mortality:
18 deaths per 1000 live births
(average annual number of deaths of infants under one year old)

AGE STRUCTURE

MEDIAN AGE is the age that divides a population in two – half the people are younger than this age, and half are older.

Median age for North America

Total population:	35.5 years
Male:	35 years
Female:	36 years

Median age for Central America

Total population:	28.5 years
Male:	28 years
Female:	29 years

Age structure
These charts show the age structure of the populations of some of the countries of North and Central America.

Key
0-14
15-64
65+

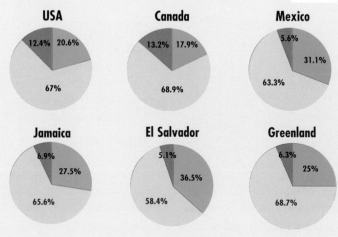

USA: 12.4% 20.6% 67%
Canada: 13.2% 17.9% 68.9%
Mexico: 5.6% 31.1% 63.3%
Jamaica: 6.9% 27.5% 65.6%
El Salvador: 5.1% 36.5% 58.4%
Greenland: 6.3% 25% 68.7%

POPULATION GROWTH

Population growth rates per year in North America:

USA	0.92%
Canada	0.9%
Greenland	− 0.02%

Highest population growth rates per year in Central America:

Turks and Caicos Islands	2.9%
Cayman Islands	2.64%
Guatemala	2.57%
Belize	2.33%
Haiti	2.26%

Alaska and Hawaii are both states within the United States of America.

North American countries total populations:

USA	295,734,134
Canada	32,805,041
Greenland	56,375
Saint Pierre & Miquelon	7012

Central American countries with highest populations:

Mexico	106,202,903
Guatemala	14,655,189
Cuba	11,346,670
Dominican Republic	8,950,034
Haiti	8,121,622

Central American countries with lowest populations:

Saint Kitts and Nevis	38,958
British Virgin Islands	22,643
Turks and Caicos Islands	20,556
Anguilla	13,254
Montserrat	9,341

For Bermuda see map above.

Central America includes the islands of the Caribbean.

60,000 to 12,000 years ago
Paleo-Indians from Siberia move into North America via Alaska. Over time, the first Americans settle into tribes, practise religions and develop cultures.

1497 — John Cabot
In 1497, John Cabot, an Italian navigator exploring for the English, is the first recorded European to land in Canada. The English later make claims to Canada. North America opens up to traders and colonizers from Europe.

1530s-1540s — Cartier
French explorer and navigator, Jacques Cartier, charts much of Canada's waters claiming areas of Canada for France.

1500s – Indigenous peoples
Most Indigenous American tribes in both Canada and the USA want at first to trade with the Europeans, but many tribes are wiped out by diseases brought by the Europeans. Many are also killed in skirmishes over land rights.

1600s – Trade & slaves
The Dutch, French, Spanish and English all trade in the USA. The English end up controlling the USA. The trade in slaves from Africa to North America grows. Slavery will exist up to the late 1800s.

1700s-1800s Colonisation
Under British rule and as an independent state the USA is often in conflict over borders and territory with both Canada and Mexico. Denmark begins to colonise Greenland.

1775 — American Revolution
The *War of Independence* begins when 13 of Britain's colonies in America seek independence. The war will last until 1783.

1776 — 4th July
Americans make *'Declaration of Independence'*.

1848 – Gold rush
Gold is discovered in California. Over the next five years, 80,000 people will head west to get rich.

• THE TIMELINE continues on page 16.

PEOPLE *of* NORTH AMERICA

THE 50 STATES OF THE USA

The United States of America is made up of 50 states.

The first 13 states were former British colonies. They were united in 1776. The final two states to join the Union were Alaska and Hawaii in 1959.

The bald eagle is the national bird of the USA.

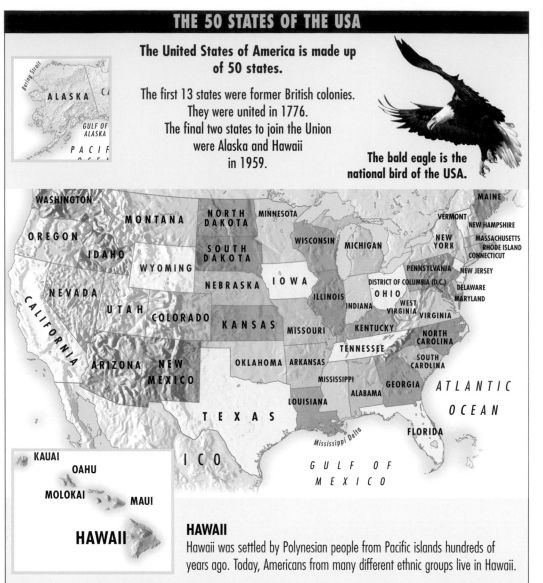

HAWAII
Hawaii was settled by Polynesian people from Pacific islands hundreds of years ago. Today, Americans from many different ethnic groups live in Hawaii.

STATE	POPULATION	CAPITAL	STATE	POPULATION	CAPITAL	STATE	POPULATION	CAPITAL
Alabama	4,500,752	Montgomery	Louisiana	4,496,334	Baton Rouge	Ohio	11,435,798	Columbus
Alaska	648,818	Juneau	Maine	1,305,728	Augusta	Oklahoma	3,511,532	Oklahoma City
Arizona	5,580,811	Phoenix	Maryland	5,508,909	Annapolis	Oregon	3,559,596	Salem
Arkansas	2,725,714	Little Rock	Massachusetts	6,433,422	Boston	Pennsylvania	12,365,455	Harrisburg
California	35,484,453	Sacramento	Michigan	10,079,985	Lansing	Rhode Island	1,076,164	Providence
Colorado	4,550,688	Denver	Minnesota	5,059,375	St. Paul	South Carolina	4,147,152	Columbia
Connecticut	3,483,372	Hartford	Mississippi	2,881,281	Jackson	South Dakota	764,309	Pierre
Delaware	817,491	Dover	Missouri	5,704,484	Jefferson City	Tennessee	5,841,748	Nashville
Florida	17,019,068	Tallahassee	Montana	917,621	Helena	Texas	22,118,509	Austin
Georgia	8,684,715	Atlanta	Nebraska	1,739,291	Lincoln	Utah	2,351,467	Salt Lake City
Hawaii	1,257,608	Honolulu	Nevada	2,241,154	Carson City	Vermont	619,107	Montpelier
Idaho	1,366,332	Boise	New Hampshire	1,287,687	Concord	Virginia	7,386,330	Richmond
Illinois	12,653,544	Springfield	New Jersey	8,638,396	Trenton	Washington	6,131,445	Olympia
Indiana	6,195,643	Indianapolis	New Mexico	1,874,614	Santa Fe	West Virginia	1,810,354	Charleston
Iowa	2,944,062	Des Moines	New York	19,190,115	Albany	Wisconsin	5,472,299	Madison
Kansas	2,723,507	Topeka	North Carolina	8,407,248	Raleigh	Wyoming	501,242	Cheyenne
Kentucky	4,117,827	Frankfort	North Dakota	633,837	Bismarck		(U.S. Census Bureau: Population, 2003 estimate.)	

ANNUAL INCOME (PER PERSON)

USA	£22,500
Canada	£17,700
Greenland	£11,250
St Pierre & Miquelon	£3,950

INTERNET USERS

COUNTRY	INTERNET USERS
USA	159,000,000
Canada	16,110,000
Greenland	20,000

LITERACY RATE

The literacy rate is the number of people aged 15 or over who can read and write. In North America the literacy rate is over 97%.

USA POVERTY FACT

In the United States of America 12% of the population live below the poverty line.

- *See GLOSSARY for a definition of POVERTY LINE.*

PEOPLE OF QUEBEC CITY

Canada is a country of English and French-speaking cultures. Quebec City is in the southeast of Canada.

Most of Quebec's residents are French-speaking.

Vieux Quebec (the old city) was made a *World Heritage site* in 1985. It is a maze of streets, ramparts, churches and battlefields – it is the oldest city in North America, and the only fortified city.

Many people in Quebec city are employed in the tourist industry – 4 million tourists visit the city every year.

In January, Quebec's residents enjoy the Winter Carnival. There are ice sculptures, dances and dog-sled races.

People statistic: *167,000 people live in Quebec City.*

THE INUIT OF NUNAVUT

A young Inuit girl keeps warm in traditional fur clothing

The Inuit live in a part of the Canadian Northwest Territories called *Nunavut*, which means *'our land'* in Inuktitut, the Inuit language.

Inuit people live modern lives in lots of ways, using snowmobiles, telephones and computers.

But some Inuit families, with government help, have chosen to become full-time hunters. They live in camps out on the ice – combining some modern comforts with a more traditional way of life.

The Inuit hunt seals, walruses, whales and wild reindeer for meat and fur.

Inuit people do not live in igloos, these are only temporary snow shelters built by hunters –

although igloo does mean 'house' in Inuktitut.

Lifestyle fact: *Inuit hunters talk to each other using radios. They call them uvaq, which means 'over' – a word the Inuit regularly heard during radio transmissions.*

The inner walls of this igloo shelter are covered in snow, which melts and freezes into a smooth covering of ice. A modern pressure lamp provides light and heat inside.

NORTH AMERICA TIMELINE

1861 – American Civil War
Abraham Lincoln becomes President of the USA. Civil War begins when Southern Confederates want to leave the Union and retain slavery. Northern Unionists under Lincoln want an end to slave labour.

1865 – Lincoln assassinated
End of American Civil War and slavery abolished in the USA. Lincoln is assassinated.

1867 – Canada Independence
In Canada, the *British North American Act* establishes Canada as a self-governing country.

1929 – US stock market crash
Stock market crash in 1929 leads to the Great Depression; investment in businesses falls; many lose jobs.

1941 – World War II
USA enters World War II after US naval base at Pearl Harbor, Hawaii, is attacked by Japan.

1950s – Korean war
The USA fights a political battle against communist states such as the USSR. This leads to actual war in Korea. The USA joins the war on the side of South Korea.

1953 – Greenland
Greenland is formally made a part of Denmark.

1965-73 – Vietnam war
The USA gives military support to South Vietnam against communist North Vietnam. USA and South Vietnam lose the war.

1969 – Man on the Moon
American Neil Armstrong becomes the first man to walk on the Moon on 20th July.

1980 – Greenland
Greenland becomes independent. Denmark controls foreign affairs.

1982 – Canada
New Constitution and Charter of Rights in Canada.

2001 – September 11th
Terrorist attacks in the USA lead to the death of nearly 3000 people.

2003 – War in Iraq
USA and Britain attack Iraq to remove its leader, Saddam Hussein.

PEOPLE
of NORTH AMERICA

Greenland is the world's largest island. Greenlanders are descended from Inuit groups and Scandinavians.

Most Greenlanders live in towns along the southwestern fringe of the island. Although there are roads, most long-distance journeys are made by air.

The fishing industry provides 95% of Greenland's income — there are more than 200 species of fish and other seafood in the island's waters.

Greenlanders shop in supermarkets where meat from seals and whales is sold alongside beef and lamb.

Culture fact: *Greenland's national costume has trousers for women worn with high boots — white boots for young girls, red for married women and blue or yellow for older women.*

CREE OF CANADA AND THE USA

The Cree live in Canada, in Manitoba and Saskatchewan, and in the USA, in Montana and North Dakota.

The Cree have two main lifestyle traditions — the Forests and the Plains. Cree first lived in forests and wooded swamps, where they hunted, fished and trapped. Many still do today. By 1800, Cree bands (groups) had moved onto the Plains to hunt buffalo.

Cree bands (groups) hold *'Walking Out'* ceremonies for children to mark the importance of their heritage. The children walk out of ceremonial tipis in their Cree costume, carrying symbolic tools or goods.

A young Cree boy dressed in traditional costume.

People statistic: *there are 200,000 Cree people, and 100,000 Metis, who have Cree and French-Canadian ancestry.*

LIFE IN NEW YORK CITY

New York is the USA's centre for finance, communications, culture and fashion. Many New Yorkers work in these sectors.

People from all over the world have migrated to the USA, arriving by ship in New York. As they sailed into New York harbour, they passed the city's most famous landmark — *The Statue of Liberty*, a symbol of freedom and hope.

New Yorkers enjoy some famous parades, such as the *Macy's Thanksgiving Parade* and *African-American Day Parade*. During *Tickertape parades* millions of paper streamers fly from the windows of buildings onto the parade below.

People fact: *New York has the largest city population in the USA — over 8 million people.*

• *See THE GLOSSARY for New York TICKERTAPE PARADES*

NEW ORLEANS

New Orleans in Louisiana State nestles along a huge bend in the great Mississippi River. In this sultry, swampy area, African, French, Creole, Cajun and Spanish cultures have blended to create an exciting mix of art, musical styles, festivals and cuisine.

On 29 August, 2005, this low-lying city was struck by Hurricane Katrina and suffered devastating flooding. Many lives were lost. Eighty per cent of the city lay under water.

Miraculously, Preservation Hall in the French Quarter survived — a symbol of the city's music traditions, such as jazz.

Before the hurricane the people of New Orleans were famous for their fantastic Mardi Gras festival held every year to celebrate the beginning of Christian Lent.

Culture fact: *every year the Krewes (competitive carnival teams) parade fabulous Mardi Gras floats and costumes. It takes the Krewes a year to prepare and all the work is done in secret.*

A Mardi Gras float.

The 93-metre-tall Statue of Liberty was erected in 1886. It was a gift from France.

THE NAVAJO NATION

The Navajo live in northeastern Arizona and adjoining parts of New Mexico and Utah states. The Navajo have been livestock farmers (with some agriculture) for hundreds of years.

The Navajo govern their affairs through an elected Navajo Nation Council, formed in 1923.

Navajo traditions include respect for nature, especially water and wind. They trace their origins to the goddess Esdzanadlehi (changing woman).

Navajo arts and crafts include fine silver work jewellery and woven rugs. These are sold to tourists, who visit the Navajo Reserve.

People statistic: *over 250,000 Navajo live in a 26,000-square-mile reservation.*

Navajo weavers work from traditional patterns which they learn as children.

• See THE GLOSSARY for information on AMERICAN INDIAN RESERVATIONS.

PEOPLE OF SAN FRANCISCO

San Francisco lies on the west coast of the USA, in California. It is often described as "49 square miles of fun"!

Many of San Francisco's 776,000 people work in the tourist and leisure industries.

San Franciscans show their enthusiasm for the future, technology and public education through the *Exploratorium* – a science, technology, nature and art museum with 600 exhibits, many of them interactive.

Many San Franciscans are huge sports fans. The city is home to the famous San Francisco 49ers National Football League team and San Francisco Giants' Major League Baseball team.

Culture Fact: *San Franciscans are well known for setting trends. In the 1960s it was Flower Power. In the 1990s, rave parties!*

FARMERS OF THE MIDWEST

There are more than 2 million farms in the United States of America. In America's midwest, the most important crops are corn, soya beans and wheat.

Farmers in the midwest grow over a third of all the corn produced in the world.

Wheat is grown in 42 states in the USA, but Kansas is the leading producer. It is known as the 'wheat state'.

In an average year, Kansas wheat farmers produce enough wheat to supply every person in the world with six loaves of bread!

Lifestyle fact: *the state of Wisconsin is sometimes called 'Dairyland'. It is America's leading producer of milk and cheese. There are as many cows in Wisconsin as there are people!*

Harvesting the wheat crop.

NORTH AMERICA FACTFILES

North America

Each country by country factfile contains: **life expectancy** and **infant mortality** figures (important indicators of quality of life and general health); **ethnic groups** and **religions** (shown as a percentage of the population, where figures are available); **main languages spoken** (listed in order of number of speakers); and the **top five industries** ranked by the amount of money they produce for the country each year.

CANADA

Total population: 32,805,041
Life expectancy (total population): 80 years
Infant mortality (per 1000 live births): 5 deaths
Ethnic mix: British origin 28%; French origin 23%; other European 15%; Amerindian 2%; mixed background 26%; others 6%
Religions: Roman Catholic 42.6%; Protestant 23.3%; other Christian 4.4%; Muslim 1.9%; others 11.8%; no religion 16%
Languages: English; French
Industries (top 5): transport equipment; chemicals; processed and unprocessed minerals; food production; timber and paper products

GREENLAND

Total population: 56,375
Life expectancy (total population): 70 years
Infant mortality (per 1000 live births): 16 deaths
Ethnic mix: Greenlander 88% (Inuit and Greenland-born white); Danish and others 12%
Religions: Evangelical Lutheran
Languages: Greenlandic (Inuit mixed with Danish); Danish; English
Industries (top 5): Fish processing; mining (gold, niobium, tantalite, uranium, iron, diamonds); handicrafts; hides and skins; ship yards

SAINT PIERRE AND MIQUELON

Total population: 7012
Life expectancy (total population): 78 years
Infant mortality (per 1000 live births): 7.5 deaths
Ethnic mix: Basques; Bretons
Religions: Roman Catholic
Languages: Creole
Industries: Fish processing; fishing; tourism
• *(Saint Pierre and Miquelon is the last remaining French-owned North American territory. It is to the east of Canada, south of Newfoundland.)*

UNITED STATES OF AMERICA

Total population: 295,734,134
Life expectancy (total population): 78 years
Infant mortality (per 1000 live births): 6.5 deaths
Ethnic mix: White 81.7%; black 12.9; Asian 4.2%; Amerindian and Alaska native 1%; native Hawaiian/Pacific islander 0.2%
Religions: Protestant 52%; Roman Catholic 24%; Mormon 2%; Jewish 1%; Muslim 1%; others 10%; no religion 10%
Languages: English; Spanish
Industries (top 5): Petroleum; steel; motor vehicles; aerospace; telecommunications

• See THE GLOSSARY for the ethnic groups, religions and languages in these FACTFILES.

c1000 BC – Olmecs
The Olmec civilisation of Mexico and Central America carve giant stone heads that weigh 18 tonnes.

1500 BC–AD 900 – Mayas
The Mayas of southern Mexico and Central America build cities and stone pyramids.

• See page 21 THE MAYA

1300 – Aztecs
The Aztec Empire is founded, with the capital, Tenochtitlan, on the site of modern-day Mexico City. The city of Tenochtitlan ruled over 500 small states of around 5.5 million people.

1492 – Christopher Columbus
Columbus lands in The Bahamas. Caribbean opened up to Spanish, French, Dutch and English colonists.

1500s – Caribbean islands
The Caribbean islands are already settled with peoples from the southern American mainland, such as the Arawaks in the western Caribbean and the Caribs in east.

1517-1521 – Cortes
Spanish explorers discover Aztecs and the gold. The Aztecs think Spanish explorer, Hernando Cortes, is the Aztec god, Quetzalcoatl. Cortes captures and kills the Aztec ruler, Montezuma II. In 1521, Spanish troops, with help from the Aztecs' local enemies, capture Tenochtitlan bringing the Aztec empire to an end.

from 1520s — Colonisation
Spanish troops kill many indigenous people in Central America. European diseases kill thousands more. Spain takes natural resources from the region and builds towns and cities.

from 1600s – Slavery
African slaves are brought by European slave traders to work on large sugar plantations on the Caribbean islands. The Islands become colonies of France, Spain and England.

• THE TIMELINE continues on page 21.

POPULATION BELOW POVERTY LINE

Many people in Central America live below the poverty line. The countries with the highest percentage of their population living in poverty are:

Haiti	80%
Guatemala	75%
Honduras	53%
Nicaragua	50%
El Salvador	36.1%

• See GLOSSARY for a definition of POVERTY LINE.

INTERNET USERS

COUNTRY	INTERNET USERS
Mexico	10,033,000
Costa Rica	800,000
Jamaica/Puerto Rico	600,000
El Salvador	550,000
Dominican Republic	500,000
Guatemala	400,000
Honduras	168,600
Trinidad & Tobago	138,000
Cuba/Panama	120,000
Barbados	100,000

• This list represents the Central American countries with the highest number of Internet users.

PEOPLE
of CENTRAL AMERICA

LIFE IN JAMAICA

Jamaica is one of the larger Caribbean islands. Its main industry is tourism.

Many Jamaicans work in hotels, shops and restaurants serving the tourist industry.

The other major industries are growing sugar cane and coffee.

Jamaican food is usually quite spicy. The national dish is Ackee (a type of fruit) with saltfish (codfish). This dish is often eaten at breakfast.

Jamaica's official language is English, but most people speak *patois* a sing-song combination of English, Spanish, Portuguese, African and Jamaican slang!

Culture fact: *reggae music comes from Jamaica. It first developed there in the 1960s.*

• See page 11 RELIGION TIMELINE for information on Rastafarianism

A Rastafarian family in Jamaica. Jamaican Rastas are descendants of African slaves. Rastafarian men wear their hair in dreadlocks, and many people wear red, green, gold and black, which symbolise blood, herbs, royalty and being African.

ANNUAL INCOME (PER PERSON)

This chart gives an overview of the average annual income per person in 10 Central American countries. It ranges from the highest income to the lowest.

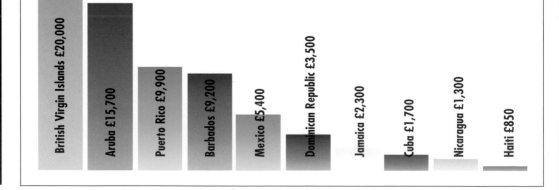

- British Virgin Islands £20,000
- Aruba £15,700
- Puerto Rico £9,900
- Barbados £9,200
- Mexico £5,400
- Dominican Republic £3,500
- Jamaica £2,300
- Cuba £1,700
- Nicaragua £1,300
- Haiti £850

MEXICO

Mexico has a mixture of peoples and traditions. Spanish language and architecture dominate Mexico, but ancient Maya and Aztec architecture and crafts still survive.

The Mexican *Day of the Dead* takes place on All Souls' Day in November.

According to ancient beliefs, on this day the dead come back to visit their loved ones.

People visit graves with candles, flowers and food, such as tombstone-shaped cakes!

Markets and shops sell skulls and skeletons made from bread or sugar.

People statistic: *19 million people live in Mexico City (Mexico's capital). It is the largest city in North and Central America.*

Skulls and coffins made of sugar for 'Día de los muertos'.

THE EMBERA TRIBE

A young Embera girl

The Embera tribe have lived for thousands of years in the Panama forests. They live by fishing, hunting, gathering food from the jungle and growing crops, such as bananas, rice and beans.

Embera are master craftsmen, famed for their baskets and high quality woodcarvings. Embera artworks are inspired by the plants and creatures of the forest — some artists have won UNESCO prizes in native handicraft competitions.

Some Embera craft items are sold to tourists, but Embera skills are mostly reserved for making their own canoes, paddles, furniture and ceremonial items, such as drums.

Lifestyle fact: *Embera know the medicinal properties of many plants, including the birth control effects of yams.*

Embera basketwork

Embera canoes

THE MAYA

With a written history, a calendar, complex laws and a system of mathematics, the ancient Maya people (1500BC–AD900) were one of the most sophisticated civilisations that ever existed.

Today there are around 6 million Mayan people living mainly in southern Mexico.

Typical Mayan houses are made of plaster and wood, and wattle and daub (rubble and clay). They have thatched roofs.

The Mayans grow maize and some vegetables. Maize forms a major part of their diet — it is baked, boiled, made into bread, or eaten as tortillas.

Culture fact: *in the village of Amatenango in Mexico, Mayan women have worked for centuries as potters using the local terra cotta (fired earth) clay.*

CENTRAL AMERICA TIMELINE

1804 – Haiti independence
After years of struggle by Haiti's slaves, Haiti becomes the first Caribbean island to declare its freedom from colonial rule by the French.

1810 – Mexican independence
Catholic priest Miguel Hidalgo, begins the struggle for Mexican independence from Spain.

1821-1823 Independence
Spanish control over Central America begins to loosen. Countries gain independence. The *United Provinces of Central America* is formed by El Salvador, Guatemala, Honduras, Nicaragua and Costa Rica.

1846-48 – Mexican War
Mexico is at war with the USA. The USA gains a lot of Mexican land after the war.

1903 – Panama independence
Following independence from Spain in 1821, Panama became a state within *Gran Colombia*. In 1903, Panama gains independence from Colombia.

1914 – Panama Canal
The USA and French-built Panama Canal is opened linking the Atlantic and Pacific Oceans.

1960s-80s – New states
Independence is gained by many Central American countries: Jamaica and Trinidad and Tobago (1962); Guyana (1966); Grenada (1974); Suriname (1975); Dominica (1978); St Lucia (1979); Belize (1981).

1998 – Hurricane Mitch
Honduras is devastated by Hurricane Mitch – 5,600 are killed and there is around $2 billion of damage. El Salvador, Nicaragua and Guatemala also suffer many deaths and losses of homes and infrastructure.

2000 to present
Central America tackling issues of slow-growing economies, inflation and pressures on the ecology of the region.

CENTRAL AMERICA
FACTFILES

North America

Central America

South America

Each country by country factfile contains: **life expectancy** and **infant mortality** figures (important indicators of quality of life and general health); **ethnic groups** and **religions** (shown as a percentage of the population, where figures are available); **main languages spoken** (listed in order of number of speakers); **literacy rates** (which, where available, can be used to compare the quality of education from country to country); and the **top five industries** ranked by the amount of money they produce for the country each year.

• See THE GLOSSARY for the ethnic groups, religions, languages and industries in these FACTFILES.

ANGUILLA
Total population: 13,254
Life expectancy (total population): 77 years
Infant mortality (per 1000 live births): 21 deaths
Ethnic mix: Black 90.1%; mixed/mulatto 4.6%; white 3.7%; others 1.6%
Religions: Christian 90.5%; others 9.5%
Languages: English
Literacy rate – male: 95% / **female:** 95%
Industries: Tourism; boat building; offshore financial services

ANTIGUA AND BARBUDA
Total population: 68,722
Life expectancy (total population): 72 years
Infant mortality (per 1000 live births): 19 deaths
Ethnic mix: Black; British; Portuguese; Lebanese; Syrian
Religions: Christianity
Languages: English; local dialects
Literacy rate – male: 90% / **female:** 88%
Industries: Tourism; construction; light manufacturing (clothing, alcohol and household appliances)

ARUBA
Total population: 71,566
Life expectancy (total population): 79 years
Infant mortality (per 1000 live births): 6 deaths
Ethnic mix: Mixed white/Caribbean/Amerindian 80%; others 20%
Religions: Roman Catholic 82%; Protestant 8%; others (including Hindu, Muslim, Confucian and Jewish) 10%
Languages: Dutch; Papiamento; English (widely spoken)
Industries: Tourism; shipping facilities; oil refining

BAHAMAS (THE)
Total population: 301,790
Life expectancy (total population): 65.5 years
Infant mortality (per 1000 live births): 25 deaths
Ethnic mix: Black 85%; white 12%; Asian and Hispanic 3%
Religions: Christian 96.3%; others 3.7%
Languages: English; Creole
Literacy rate – male: 94.7% / **female:** 96.5%
Industries (top 5): Tourism; banking; cement; oil shipping; salt

BARBADOS
Total population: 279,254
Life expectancy (total population): 71 years
Infant mortality (per 1000 live births): 12.5 deaths
Ethnic mix: Black 90%; white 4%; Asian and mixed 6%
Religions: Protestant 67%; Roman Catholic 4%; no religion 17%; others 12%
Languages: English
Literacy rate – male: 98% / **female:** 96.8%
Industries: Tourism; sugar; some manufacturing and component assembly for export

BELIZE
Total population: 279,457
Life expectancy (total population): 67.5 years
Infant mortality (per 1000 live births): 26 deaths
Ethnic mix: Mestizo 48.7%; Creole 24.9%; Maya 10.6%; others 15.8%
Religions: Roman Catholic 49.6%; Protestant 27%; others 14%; no religion 9.4%
Languages: English; Spanish; Mayan
Literacy rate – male: 94.1% / **female:** 94.1%
Industries: Clothing production; food processing; tourism; construction

BERMUDA
Total population: 63,365
Life expectancy (total population): 78 years
Infant mortality (per 1000 live births): 8.5 deaths
Ethnic mix: Black 54.8%; white 34.1%; others 11.1%
Religions: Christian 67%; others 19%; no religion 14%
Languages: English; Portuguese
Literacy rate – male: 98% / **female:** 99%
Industries: Tourism; light manufacturing

BRITISH VIRGIN ISLANDS
Total population: 22,643
Life expectancy (total population): 76 years
Infant mortality (per 1000 live births): 18 deaths
Ethnic mix: Black 83%; others (including white, Indian, Asian and mixed) 17%
Religions: Protestant 86%; Roman Catholic 10%; others 2%; no religion 2%
Languages: English
Industries (top 5): Tourism; light industry; construction; rum; concrete block manufacturing

CAYMAN ISLANDS
Total population: 44,270
Life expectancy (total population): 80 years
Infant mortality (per 1000 live births): 8 deaths
Ethnic mix: Mixed 40%; white 20%; black 20%; others 20%
Religions: Christianity
Languages: English
Literacy rate – male: 98% / **female:** 98%
Industries (top 5): Tourism; banking; insurance and finance; construction; construction materials

COSTA RICA
Total population: 4,016,173
Life expectancy (total population): 77 years
Infant mortality (per 1000 live births): 10 deaths
Ethnic mix: White and Mestizo 94%; black 3%; Amerindian 1%; Chinese 1%; others 1%
Religions: Roman Catholic 76.3%; Protestant 14.4%; others 6.1%; no religion 3.2%
Languages: Spanish; English
Literacy rate – male: 95.9% / **female:** 96.1%
Industries (top 5): Microprocessors; food processing; textiles; construction materials; fertiliser

CUBA
Total population: 11,346,670
Life expectancy (total population): 77 years
Infant mortality (per 1000 live births): 6 deaths
Ethnic mix: Mulatto 51%; white 37%; black 11%; Chinese 1%
Religions: Christianity; Judaism; Santeria
Languages: Spanish
Literacy rate – male: 97.2% / **female:** 96.9%
Industries (top 5): Sugar; petroleum; tobacco; construction; nickel

DOMINICA
Total population: 69,029
Life expectancy (total population): 75 years
Infant mortality (per 1000 live births): 14 deaths
Ethnic mix: Black; mixed black/European; European; Syrian; Carib Amerindian
Religions: Roman Catholic 77%; Protestant 15%; others 6%; no religion 2%
Languages: English; French patois
Literacy rate – male: 94% / **female:** 94%
Industries (top 5): Soap; coconut oil; tourism; copra; furniture

DOMINICAN REPUBLIC
Total population: 8,950,034
Life expectancy (total population): 67 years
Infant mortality (per 1000 live births): 32 deaths
Ethnic mix: White 16%; black 11%; mixed 73%
Religions: Roman Catholic 95%; others 5%
Languages: Spanish
Literacy rate – male: 84.6% / **female:** 84.8%
Industries (top 5): Tourism; sugar processing; mining (ferronickel and gold); textiles; cement

EL SALVADOR
Total population: 6,704,932
Life expectancy (total population): 71 years
Infant mortality (per 1000 live births): 25 deaths
Ethnic mix: Mestizo 90%; white 9%; Amerindian 1%
Religions: Roman Catholic 83%; others (including Protestant) 17%
Languages: Spanish; Nahua
Literacy rate – male: 82.8% / **female:** 77.7%
Industries (top 5): Food processing; drinks production; petroleum; chemicals; fertiliser

GRENADA
Total population: 89,502
Life expectancy (total population): 64.5 years
Infant mortality (per 1000 live births): 15 deaths
Ethnic mix: Black 82%; black/European 13%; others 5%
Religions: Christianity
Languages: English; French patois
Literacy rate – male: 98% / **female:** 98%
Industries (top 5): Food and drinks production; textiles; light assembly operations; tourism; construction

GUADELOUPE

Total population: 448,713
Life expectancy (total population): 78 years
Infant mortality (per 1000 live births): 9 deaths
Ethnic mix: Black or mulatto 90%; white 5%; others (including East Indian, Lebanese and Chinese) 5%
Religions: Roman Catholic 95%; others (including Hindu, pagan African religions and Protestant) 5%
Languages: French
Literacy rate – male: 90% / **female:** 90%
Industries (top 5): Construction; cement; rum; sugar; tourism

GUATEMALA

Total population: 14,655,189
Life expectancy (total population): 65 years
Infant mortality (per 1000 live births): 36 deaths
Ethnic mix: Mestizo and European 59.4%; Mayan 40.3%; others 0.3%
Religions: Christian; indigenous Mayan beliefs
Languages: Spanish; Amerindian languages including Quiche, Cakchiquel, Kekchi, Mam, Garifuna and Xinca
Literacy rate – male: 78% / **female:** 63.3%
Industries (top 5): Sugar; textiles; furniture; chemicals; petroleum

HAITI

Total population: 8,121,622
Life expectancy (total population): 53 years
Infant mortality (per 1000 live births): 73 deaths
Ethnic mix: Black 95%; mulatto and white 5%
Religions: Roman Catholic 80%; Protestant 16%; others 4%; approximately 50% of the population also practise Voodoo
Languages: French; Creole
Literacy rate – male: 54.8% / **female:** 51.2%
Industries (top 5): Sugar refining; flour milling; textiles; cement; light assembly industries based on imported components

HONDURAS

Total population: 6,975,204
Life expectancy (total population): 66 years
Infant mortality (per 1000 live births): 29 deaths
Ethnic mix: Mestizo 90%; Amerindian 7%; black 2%; white 1%
Religions: Roman Catholic 97%; Protestant 3%
Languages: Spanish; Amerindian dialects
Literacy rate – male: 76.1% / **female:** 76.3%
Industries: Sugar; coffee; textiles; timber products

JAMAICA

Total population: 2,731,832
Life expectancy (total population): 76 years
Infant mortality (per 1000 live births): 12 deaths
Ethnic mix: Black 90.9%; East Indian 1.3%; white 0.2%; Chinese 0.2%; mixed 7.3%; others 0.1%
Religions: Christian 65.3%; others (including spiritual cults) 34.7%
Languages: English; English patois
Literacy rate – male: 84.1% / **female:** 91.6%
Industries (top 5): Tourism; bauxite/alumina industries; textiles; agro processing; light manufacturing

MARTINIQUE

Total population: 432,900
Life expectancy (total population): 79 years
Infant mortality (per 1000 live births): 7 deaths
Ethnic mix: African and mixed African, white and Indian 90%; white 5%; others 5%
Religions: Roman Catholic 85%; Protestant 10.5%; Muslim 0.5%; Hindu 0.5%; others 3.5%
Languages: French; creole patois
Literacy rate – male: 97.4% / **female:** 98.1%
Industries (top 5): Construction; rum; cement; oil refining; sugar

MEXICO

Total population: 106,202,903
Life expectancy (total population): 75 years
Infant mortality (per 1000 live births): 21 deaths
Ethnic mix: Mestizo 60%; Amerindian 30%; white 9%; others 1%
Religions: Roman Catholic 89%; Protestant 6%; others 5%
Languages: Spanish; Mayan; Nahuatl and other indigenous languages
Literacy rate – male: 94% / **female:** 90.5%
Industries (top 5): Food and drinks production; tobacco; chemicals; iron and steel; petroleum

MONTSERRAT

Total population: 9,341
Life expectancy (total population): 79 years
Infant mortality (per 1000 live births): 7 deaths
Ethnic mix: Black; white
Religions: Christianity
Languages: English
Literacy rate – male: 97% / **female:** 97%
Industries: Tourism; rum; textiles; electronic appliances

NICARAGUA

Total population: 5,465,100
Life expectancy (total population): 70 years
Infant mortality (per 1000 live births): 29 deaths
Ethnic mix: Mestizo 69%; white 17%; black 9%; Amerindian 5%
Religions: Roman Catholic 72.9%; Protestant 16.7%; others 1.9%; no religion 8.5%
Languages: Spanish
Literacy rate – male: 67.2% / **female:** 67.8%
Industries (top 5): Food processing; chemicals; machinery and metal products; textiles; petroleum refining and distribution

PANAMA

Total population: 3,039,150
Life expectancy (total population): 72 years
Infant mortality (per 1000 live births): 20 deaths
Ethnic mix: Mestizo 70%; Amerindian and West Indian 14%; white 10%; Amerindian 6%
Religions: Roman Catholic 85%; Protestant 15%
Languages: Spanish; English
Literacy rate – male: 93.2% / **female:** 91.9%
Industries: Construction; brewing; cement and construction materials; sugar milling

PUERTO RICO

Total population: 3,916,632
Life expectancy (total population): 78 years
Infant mortality (per 1000 live births): 8 deaths
Ethnic mix: White (mostly Spanish origin) 80.5%; black 8%; Amerindian 0.4%; Asian 0.2%; mixed and others 10.9%
Religions: Roman Catholic 85%; Protestant and others 15%
Languages: Spanish; English
Literacy rate – male: 93.7% / **female:** 94.4%
Industries (top 5): Pharmaceuticals; electronics; clothing; food production; tourism

ST KITTS AND NEVIS

Total population: 38,958
Life expectancy (total population): 72 years
Infant mortality (per 1000 live births): 14.5 deaths
Ethnic mix: Black; some British, Portuguese and Lebanese
Religions: Christianity
Languages: English
Literacy rate – male: 97% / **female:** 98%
Industries (top 5): Sugar processing; tourism; cotton; salt; copra

ST LUCIA

Total population: 166,312
Life expectancy (total population): 74 years
Infant mortality (per 1000 live births): 13.5 deaths
Ethnic mix: Black 90%; mixed 6%; East Indian 3%; white 1%
Religions: Roman Catholic 67.5%; Protestant 23.3%; Rastafarian 2.1%; others 2.6%; no religion 4.5%
Languages: English; French patois
Literacy rate – male: 65% / **female:** 69%
Industries (top 5): Clothing; assembly of electronic components; drinks production; corrugated cardboard boxes; tourism

ST VINCENT AND THE GRENADINES

Total population: 117,534
Life expectancy (total population): 74 years
Infant mortality (per 1000 live births): 15 deaths
Ethnic mix: Black 66%; mixed 19%; East Indian 6%; Carib Amerindian 2%; others 7%
Religions: Christian; Hindu
Languages: English; French patois
Literacy rate – male: 96% / **female:** 96%
Industries (top 5): Food processing; cement; furniture; clothing; starch

TRINIDAD AND TOBAGO

Total population: 1,088,644
Life expectancy (total population): 69 years
Infant mortality (per 1000 live births): 24 deaths
Ethnic mix: Indian 40%; African 37.5%; mixed 20.5%; others 2%
Religions: Roman Catholic 26%; Hindu 22.5%; Protestant 23.8%; Muslim 5.8%; others 21.9%
Languages: English; Hindi; French; Spanish; Chinese
Literacy rate – male: 99% / **female:** 98%
Industries (top 5): Petroleum; chemicals; tourism; food processing; cement

TURKS AND CAICOS ISLANDS

Total population: 20,556
Life expectancy (total population): 74.5 years
Infant mortality (per 1000 live births): 16 deaths
Ethnic mix: Black 90%; others (including mixed, European and North American) 10%
Religions: Christian 86%; others 14%
Languages: English
Literacy rate – male: 99% / **female:** 98%
Industries: Tourism; offshore financial services

VIRGIN ISLANDS

Total population: 108,708
Life expectancy (total population): 79 years
Infant mortality (per 1000 live births): 8 deaths
Ethnic mix: Black 76.2%; white 13.1%; others 10.7%
Religions: Christian 93%; others 7%
Languages: English; Spanish or Spanish Creole; French or French Creole
Industries (top 5): Tourism; petroleum refining; wristwatch assembly; rum distilling; construction

Young children queue for food aid from a Christian organisation in Nicaragua – 50% of Nicaragua's population lives in poverty.

SOUTH AMERICA TIMELINE

12,000 years ago
Humans arrive in South America, walking from North and Central America.

3000 BC – First farmers
People start to grow potatoes and manioc. They domesticate llamas and guinea pigs.

AD 100 – The Moche
The Moche culture of northern Peru flourishes until AD 750. The people farm, irrigate land, hunt sea lions and make pottery and gold and silver jewellery.

AD 200 – The Nazcas
The Nazca people of southern Peru make enormous line drawings in the desert which can only be seen from the air.

1400s – The Incas
The Inca empire of the Andes begins to expand. By the end of the century, the empire will reach from Ecuador to Chile controlling 10 million people.

1492 – Christopher Columbus
Columbus crosses the Atlantic from Spain. European colonisation of the 'New World' begins.

1494 – Treaty of Tordesillas
The *Treaty of Tordesillas* draws a line on the map which vertically dissects South America. Spain will have all the land to the west, Portugal all the land to the east.

1500 – Discovering Brazil
Portuguese navigator Pedro Alvares Cabral discovers Brazil.

1600s – Slave trade
Over the next three centuries, millions of people will be taken from Africa to Brazil and other Central and South American countries to work as slaves, mainly in sugar plantations.

1500s – Catholic missions
Catholic missions to convert the indigenous people of South America to Christianity begin.

• The TIMELINE continues on page 25.

SOUTH AMERICA

Over the centuries, settlers from Europe, Africa and Asia have migrated to this continent to make lives alongside the indigenous South American peoples. Stretching down the west of South America, the vast Andes mountain range is home to millions – some people live traditional farming lives in tiny mountain villages, while others live in mountain cities, such as La Paz in Bolivia. Today, over 90% of South Americans are Roman Catholic – the religion introduced by Spanish and Portuguese invaders in the 1500s.

A Chilean farmer harvests grapes for winemaking. Chilean wines are exported all over the world.

STATISTICS: PEOPLE OF SOUTH AMERICA

Average life expectancy across continent:
Male: 70 years
Female: 76 years

Highest life expectancy:
French Guiana 77 years

Lowest life expectancy:
Guyana 65.5 years

Death rate: 6
(average annual number of deaths per 1000 people)

Birth rate: 19
(average annual number of births per 1000 people)

Total fertility rate: 2.5
(average number of children born per woman)

Infant mortality:
23 deaths per 1000 live births
(average annual number of deaths of infants under one year old)

AGE STRUCTURE

MEDIAN AGE is the age that divides a population in two – half the people are younger than this age and half are older.

Median age for South America

Total population: 27 years
Male: 26 years
Female: 27.5 years

Age structure
These charts show the age structure of the populations of three South American countries.

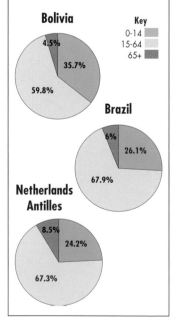

Bolivia
Key
0-14
15-64
65+
4.5%
35.7%
59.8%

Brazil
6%
26.1%
67.9%

Netherlands Antilles
8.5%
24.2%
67.3%

ANNUAL INCOME (PER PERSON)

This chart gives an overview of the average annual income per person in 10 South American countries. It ranges from the highest income to the lowest.

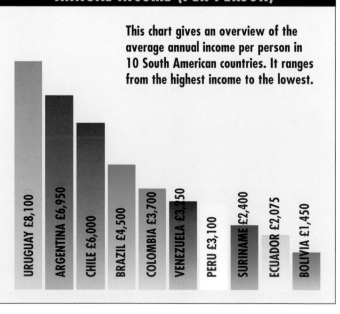

URUGUAY £8,100
ARGENTINA £6,950
CHILE £6,000
BRAZIL £4,500
COLOMBIA £3,700
VENEZUELA £3,250
PERU £3,100
SURINAME £2,400
ECUADOR £2,075
BOLIVIA £1,450

MAP OF SOUTH AMERICA

CARIBBEAN SEA

Gulf of Venezuela

LESSER ANTILLES

Netherlands Antilles

TRINIDAD & TOBAGO

PANAMA

VENEZUELA

ATLANTIC OCEAN

Gulf of Panama

GUYANA SURINAME FRENCH GUIANA

COLOMBIA

ECUADOR

Marajó Bay

Marajó Island

São Marcos Bay

Fernando de Noronha Island

Amazon

PACIFIC OCEAN

B R A Z I L

PERU

BOLIVIA

PARAGUAY

C H I L E

ATLANTIC OCEAN

ARGENTINA

URUGUAY

Blanca Bay

Valdés Peninsula

Gulf of San Jorge

West Falkland

FALKLAND/MALVINAS ISLANDS

Grande Bay

East Falkland

Strait of Magellan

South Georgia

Isla Grande

Tierra del Fuego

S C O T I A S E A

Cape Horn

TOTAL POPULATION

Total population of South America:
371,400,000

POPULATION GROWTH

Highest population growth rates per year in South America:

Paraguay	2.48%
French Guiana	2.1%
Bolivia/Colombia	1.49%
Venezuela	1.4%
Peru	1.36%

POPULATION BELOW POVERTY LINE

Suriname	70%
Bolivia	64%
Colombia	55%

• See GLOSSARY for a definition of POVERTY LINE.

INTERNET USERS

COUNTRY	INTERNET USERS
Brazil	14,300,000
Argentina	4,100,000
Chile	3,575,000
Peru	2,850,000
Colombia	2,732,200

• This list represents the South American countries with the highest number of Internet users.

COUNTRIES BY POPULATION

South American countries with highest populations:

Brazil 186,112,794

Colombia 42,954,279

Argentina 39,537,943

Peru 27,925,628

Venezuela 25,375,281

Lowest populations:

Paraguay 6,347,884

Uruguay 3,415,920

Guyana 765,283

Netherlands Antilles 219,958

French Guiana 195,506

SOUTH AMERICA TIMELINE

1532 to 1572 – End of the Inca empire
In 1532, Spanish adventurer Francisco Pizarro and his Conquistadors land on the north coast of Peru. The Spanish will conquer the Inca Empire. They will steal treasure, drive people from their villages, and kill thousands.

1667 – Suriname
The Dutch colonise Suriname and set up sugar plantations.

1811-1828 – Independence
In 1811, Venezuela declares independence from Spain, led by Simon Bolivar a Venezuelan general. Bolivar leads the struggle for independence in other South American countries. Independence from Spain comes to Argentina in 1816; Chile in 1818; Colombia and Peru in 1821; Ecuador in 1822; Bolivia in 1825; Uruguay in 1828. Brazil gains independence from Portugal in 1822. The new states are democratic republics, but during the 19th and 20th centuries there will be many revolutions, civil wars and military dictatorships.

1879-1883 – War of Pacific
Chile gains 850 kilometres of coastline from Peru and Bolivia.

1888 – Slavery in Brazil
Slavery is abolished in Brazil.

1911 – Lost Inca City
Machu Picchu, an Inca city, is discovered by American explorer Hiram Bingham.

1930 – First World Cup
Uruguay win the first football World Cup (they will also win in 1950).

1932-1935 – Chaco War
Paraguay takes the Chaco region from Bolivia in the Chaco War.

1958-1986 – World Cup
Brazil win the football World Cup in 1958. They will win again in 1962, 1970 and 1994. Argentina win the World Cup in 1978 and 1986.

2002 — Five times!
Brazil win the World Cup for the fifth time!

PEOPLE *of* SOUTH AMERICA

THE UROS OF LAKE TITICACA

At the Peruvian end of Lake Titicaca live the 800 or so Uros Indians. In the shallow waters of the lake grow hollow reeds called *tortora*. The Uros use these reeds to fulfill most of their needs.

The Uros have built around 40 small, floating islands, formed from layers of reeds.

Uros huts are also made from sheets of reeds bound together.

The tortora reeds are woven into mats which are used to make boats, and they are burned as fuel.

To accompany their meals of fish caught in the lake, the Uros eat the soft tortora hearts.

Lifestyle fact: *the Uros drink a healing tea made from the flowers of the tortora reed.*

The reeds that form the islands rot away quite quickly, so the *'ground'* has to be regularly renewed with fresh reeds.

BRAZIL AND FOOTBALL

In Brazil, football does not count as a sport – it's a religion!

Brazil has won the football World Cup five times — more often than any other country.

For young children growing up in poverty in the slums of Brazil's big cities, the dream is to be discovered by a local football club. The very best footballers go on to play for their country, and can make fortunes playing for European football clubs.

'Street children' can often be seen playing football in the public squares and on the beaches of Brazil's capital, Rio de Janeiro.

Brazilian Children play football next to the cheaply-built, slum houses, called *favelas*.

People statistic: *it is estimated that around 7 to 8 million children in Brazil live on the streets.*

PEOPLE OF THE ANDES

In the Andes mountains of Peru, small communities maintain traditional ways of life that are unchanged from those of their ancestors, the Incas who lived in this region 500 years ago.

Llamas

At altitudes of 3,600 metres, the only crops that will grow are potatoes, and around 200 varieties are grown in the Andes.

Llamas are kept for transporting potatoes and other goods from highland villages to markets.

In Inca times, textiles were more highly prized than gold or silver.

Today, women still weave colourful cloth from llama and alpaca wool. It is used to make ponchos and shawls.

Lifestyle fact: *around 13 million people in South America still speak Quechua the language of the Incas.*

A person's home village can be identified by the patterns in the textiles they wear.

THE RAINFOREST YANOMAMI

The Amazon rainforest, close to the border of Brazil and Venezuela, is home to the 20,000 Yanomami people.

The Yanomami gather fruits from the forest, grow basic crops and hunt for forest birds and animals.

Extended family groups live in huge dwellings called yanos which sometimes house up to 400 people. Each Yanomami family has its own area within the yano and everyone sleeps in hammocks, hung in layers from the ceiling.

Culture fact: *when someone dies, family and friends drink a soup made with their ground-up bones and ashes from their cremation. In this way, the deceased person becomes part of the living.*

Yanomami men put feathers in their hair and pigment on their faces as they dress as warriors for a funeral ceremony.

SOUTH AMERICA FACTFILES

South America

Each country by country factfile contains: **life expectancy** and **infant mortality** figures (important indicators of quality of life and general health); **ethnic groups** and **religions** (shown as a percentage of the population, where figures are available); **main languages spoken** (listed in order of number of speakers); **literacy rates** (which, where available, can be used to compare the quality of education from country to country); and the **top five industries** ranked by the amount of money they produce for the country each year.

> • See THE GLOSSARY for the ethnic groups, religions, languages and industries in these FACTFILES.

ARGENTINA
Total population: 39,537,943
Life expectancy (total population): 76 years
Infant mortality (per 1000 live births) : 15 deaths
Ethnic mix: White (Spanish and Italian) 97%; others (including Mestizo and Amerindian) 3%
Religions: Roman Catholic 92% (but less than 20% practising); Protestant 2%; Jewish 2%; others 4%
Languages: Spanish; English; Italian; German; French
Literacy rate – male: 97.1% / female: 97.1%
Industries (top 5): Food processing; motor vehicles; light manufacturing; textiles; chemicals and petrochemicals

BOLIVIA

Total population: 8,857,870
Life expectancy (total population): 65.5 years
Infant mortality (per 1000 live births): 53 deaths
Ethnic mix: Quechua 30%; Mestizo 30%; Aymara 25%; white 15%
Religions: Roman Catholic 95%; Protestant 5%
Languages: Spanish; Quechua; Aymara
Literacy rate – male: 93.1% / female: 81.6%
Industries (top 5): Mining; smelting metals; petroleum; food and drinks production; tobacco

BRAZIL
Total population: 186,112,794
Life expectancy (total population): 72 years
Infant mortality (per 1000 live births): 30 deaths
Ethnic mix: White 53.7%; mulatto 38.5%; black 6.2%; others 1.6%
Religions: Roman Catholic 73.6%; Protestant 15.4%; Spiritualist 1.3%; Bantu/Voodoo 0.3%; others 2%; no religion 7.4%
Languages: Portuguese; Spanish; English; French
Literacy rate – male: 86.1% / female: 86.6%
Industries (top 5): Textiles; shoes; chemicals; cement; timber

CHILE
Total population: 15,980,912
Life expectancy (total population): 76.5years
Infant mortality (per 1000 live births): 9 deaths
Ethnic mix: White and white/Amerindian 95%; Amerindian 3%; others 2%
Religions: Roman Catholic 89%; Protestant 11%
Languages: Spanish
Literacy rate – male: 96.4% / female: 96.1%
Industries (top 5): Copper and other minerals; food processing; fish processing; iron and steel; timber

COLOMBIA
Total population: 42,954,279
Life expectancy (total population): 72 years
Infant mortality (per 1000 live births): 21 deaths
Ethnic mix: Mestizo 58%; white 20%; mulatto 14%; black 4%; mixed black/Amerindian 3%; Amerindian 1%
Religions: Roman Catholic 90%; others 10%
Languages: Spanish
Literacy rate – male: 92.4% / female: 92.6%
Industries (top 5): Textiles; food processing; oil; clothing and shoes; drinks production

ECUADOR

Total population: 13,363,593
Life expectancy (total population): 76 years
Infant mortality (per 1000 live births): 24 deaths
Ethnic mix: Mestizo 65%; Amerindian 25%; others (including Spanish and black) 10%
Religions: Roman Catholic 95%; others 5%
Languages: Spanish; Quechua
Literacy rate – male: 94% / female: 91%
Industries (top 5): Petroleum; food processing; textiles; timber products; chemicals

FRENCH GUIANA

Total population: 195,506
Life expectancy (total population): 77 years
Infant mortality (per 1000 live births): 12 deaths
Ethnic mix: Black or mulatto 66%; white 12%; others (including East Indian, Chinese and Amerindian) 22%
Religions: Roman Catholic
Languages: French
Literacy rate – male: 84% / female: 82%
Industries (top 5): Construction; shrimp processing; timber products; rum; gold mining

GUYANA

Total population: 765,283
Life expectancy (total population): 65.5 years
Infant mortality (per 1000 live births): 33 deaths
Ethnic mix: East Indian 50%; black 36%; Amerindian 7%; others (including white and Chinese) 7%
Religions: Christian 50%; Hindu 35%; Muslim 10%; others 5%
Languages: English; Amerindian dialects; Creole; Hindi; Urdu
Literacy rate – male: 99.1% / female: 98.5%
Industries (top 5): Bauxite mining; sugar; rice milling; timber; textiles

NETHERLANDS ANTILLES

Total population: 219,958
Life expectancy (total population): 76 years
Infant mortality (per 1000 live births): 10 deaths
Ethnic mix: Mixed/black 85%; others including (Carib Amerindian, white and East Asian) 15%
Religions: Roman Catholic 72%; Protestant 18.6%; others 9.4%
Languages: Papiamento; English; Dutch
Literacy rate – male: 96.7% / female: 96.8%
Industries: Tourism; petroleum refining and shipping; light manufacturing

PARAGUAY

Total population: 6,347,884
Life expectancy (total population): 75 years
Infant mortality (per 1000 live births): 26 deaths
Ethnic mix: Mestizo 95%; others 5%
Religions: Roman Catholic 90%; Protestant 10%
Languages: Spanish; Guarani
Literacy rate – male: 94.9% / female: 93%
Industries (top 5): Sugar; cement; textiles; drinks production; timber products

PERU

Total population: 27,925,628
Life expectancy (total population): 70 years
Infant mortality (per 1000 live births): 32 deaths
Ethnic mix: Amerindian 45%; Mestizo 37%; white 15%; others (including black, Japanese and Chinese) 3%
Religions: Roman Catholic 81%; Protestant 2.1%; others or no religion 16.9%
Languages: Spanish; Quechua; Aymara; a large number of minor Amazonian languages
Literacy rate – male: 95.2% / female: 86.8%
Industries (top 5): Mining and refining of minerals and metals; petroleum; natural gas; fishing and fish processing; textiles

SURINAME
Total population: 438,144
Life expectancy (total population): 69 years
Infant mortality (per 1000 live births): 23.5 deaths
Ethnic mix: Hindustani (ancestors emigrated from northern India) 37%; Creole 31%; Javanese 15%; Maroons (descendants of African slaves) 10%; Amerindian 2%; others 5%
Religions: Hindu 27.4%; Protestant 25.2%; Roman Catholic 22.8%; Muslim 19.6%; indigenous beliefs 5%
Languages: Dutch; English; Sranang Tongo (sometimes called Taki–Taki, native language of Creole people)
Literacy rate – male: 95% / female: 91%
Industries (top 5): Mining (bauxite and gold); alumina production; oil; timber; food processing

URUGUAY
Total population: 3,415,920
Life expectancy (total population): 76 years
Infant mortality (per 1000 live births): 12 deaths
Ethnic mix: White 88%; mestizo 8%; black 4%
Religions: Roman Catholic 66%; Protestant 2%; Jewish 1%; others or no religion 31%
Languages: Spanish
Literacy rate – male: 97.6% / female: 98.4%
Industries (top 5): Food processing; electrical machinery; transportation equipment; petroleum products; textiles

VENEZUELA
Total population: 25,375,281
Life expectancy (total population): 74 years
Infant mortality (per 1000 live births): 22 deaths
Ethnic mix: Spanish; Italian; Portuguese; Arab; German; African; indigenous people
Religions: Roman Catholic 96%; Protestant 2%; others 2%
Languages: Spanish; numerous indigenous dialects
Literacy rate – male: 93.8% / female: 93.1%
Industries (top 5): Petroleum; iron ore mining; construction materials; food processing; textiles

TOTAL POPULATION

Total population of Africa:

887,000,000

COUNTRIES BY POPULATION

African countries with highest population:

Nigeria	128,771,988
Egypt	77,505,756
Ethiopia	73,053,286
Congo (Democratic Republic of) 60,085,804	
South Africa 44,344,136	

Lowest population:

Seychelles	81,188
Sao Tome and Principe 187,410	
Mayotte	193,633
Cape Verde 418,224	
Djibouti 476,703	

AFRICA

Africa is home to many hundreds of different peoples who practise numerous religions and live highly varied lifestyles. Africa is also home to some of the poorest people in the world. Some Africans live with drought and famine, others with civil wars and political unrest. Many African countries have large international debts to pay. However, Africa has one important resource – the young people who want to build a new future for their continent.

After 27 years of civil war, a young Angolan boy gives the sign that life is good in a peaceful Angola.

AFRICA FACTS

Angola has the world's highest rate of infant mortality: 191 deaths for every 1000 live births.

At the end of 2004, nearly 26 million adults and children in Africa were living with HIV/AIDs.

STATISTICS: PEOPLE OF AFRICA

Average life expectancy across continent:
Male: 51 years
Female: 53 years

Highest life expectancy:
Libya   76.5 years

Lowest life expectancy:
Botswana 34 years

Death rate: 15
(average annual number of deaths per 1000 people)

Birth rate: 35
(average annual number of births per 1000 people)

Total fertility rate: 5
(average number of children born per woman)

Infant mortality:
77 deaths per 1000 live births
(average annual number of deaths of infants under one year old)

AGE STRUCTURE

MEDIAN AGE is the age that divides a population in two – half the people are younger than this age and half are older.

Median age for Africa

Total population	19 years
Male:	19 years
Female:	19.5 years

War, HIV/AIDs and poverty mean many adults die young in Africa. In most African countries a large percentage of the population are children or teenagers.

Age structure
These charts show the age structure of the populations of four African countries.

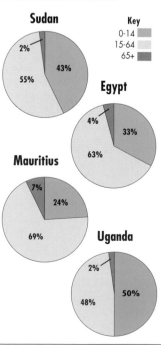

Sudan
2%
43%
55%

Key
0-14
15-64
65+

Egypt
4%
33%
63%

Mauritius
7%
24%
69%

Uganda
2%
50%
48%

ANNUAL INCOME (PER PERSON)

This chart gives an overview of the average annual income per person in 10 African countries. It ranges from the highest income to the lowest.

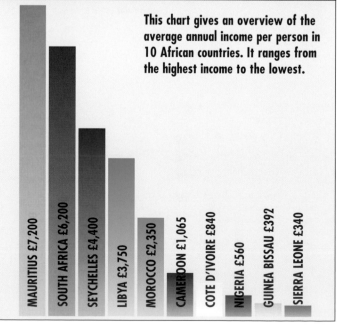

MAURITIUS £7,200
SOUTH AFRICA £6,200
SEYCHELLES £4,400
LIBYA £3,750
MOROCCO £2,350
CAMEROON £1,065
COTE D'IVOIRE £840
NIGERIA £560
GUINEA BISSAU £392
SIERRA LEONE £340

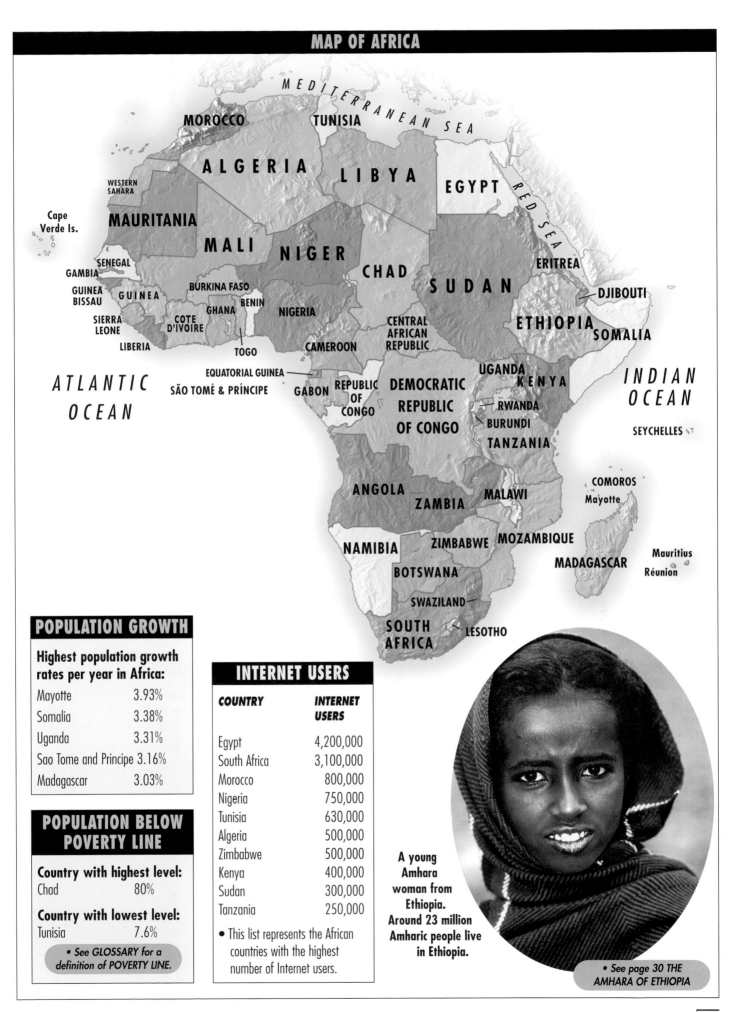

MEDITERRANEAN SEA

MOROCCO   TUNISIA

ALGERIA   LIBYA   EGYPT

WESTERN SAHARA

Cape Verde Is.

MAURITANIA   MALI   NIGER   CHAD   SUDAN   ERITREA

SENEGAL   DJIBOUTI

GAMBIA   BURKINA FASO

GUINEA BISSAU   GUINEA   BENIN   CENTRAL AFRICAN REPUBLIC   ETHIOPIA   SOMALIA

GHANA   NIGERIA

SIERRA LEONE   COTE D'IVOIRE

LIBERIA   TOGO   CAMEROON

EQUATORIAL GUINEA   UGANDA   KENYA

SÃO TOMÉ & PRÍNCIPE   GABON   REPUBLIC OF CONGO   DEMOCRATIC REPUBLIC OF CONGO   RWANDA   SEYCHELLES

ATLANTIC OCEAN   BURUNDI

TANZANIA   INDIAN OCEAN

ANGOLA   MALAWI   COMOROS

ZAMBIA   Mayotte

NAMIBIA   ZIMBABWE   MOZAMBIQUE

BOTSWANA   MADAGASCAR   Mauritius   Réunion

SWAZILAND

SOUTH AFRICA   LESOTHO

RED SEA

POPULATION GROWTH

Highest population growth rates per year in Africa:

Mayotte	3.93%
Somalia	3.38%
Uganda	3.31%
Sao Tome and Principe	3.16%
Madagascar	3.03%

POPULATION BELOW POVERTY LINE

Country with highest level:

Chad	80%

Country with lowest level:

Tunisia	7.6%

• See GLOSSARY for a definition of POVERTY LINE.

INTERNET USERS

COUNTRY	INTERNET USERS
Egypt	4,200,000
South Africa	3,100,000
Morocco	800,000
Nigeria	750,000
Tunisia	630,000
Algeria	500,000
Zimbabwe	500,000
Kenya	400,000
Sudan	300,000
Tanzania	250,000

• This list represents the African countries with the highest number of Internet users.

A young Amhara woman from Ethiopia. Around 23 million Amharic people live in Ethiopia.

• See page 30 THE AMHARA OF ETHIOPIA

AFRICA TIMELINE

1,000,000-100,000 years ago
Human beings evolve in Africa. They hunt and gather food and gradually move to other parts of the world.

5000-3000 BC – First farmers
The world's earliest farmers grow sorghum, African rice, and keep guinea fowl, in the dry grasslands south of the Sahara. People grow African yams and oil palm in the West African rainforest.

3000 BC – Ancient Egyptians
The Egyptian civilisation rises in the valley of the Nile.

2500 BC – Pyramid builders
The ancient Egyptians build the Great Pyramid at Giza, Egypt, as a tomb for Pharaoh Khufu.

30 BC – Roman Empire
Egypt becomes part of the Roman Empire, which soon includes the whole Mediterranean coast of North Africa.

641 AD – Islam
Arab invaders bring Islam to Egypt; by the early 700s they have conquered North Africa.

1235 – Empire of Mali
The Empire of Mali is established in western Sahel (semi-arid region of north and west Africa). This is the first of several black, Muslim states in this region.

1487 – Bartholomeu Dias
Portuguese explorer Bartholomeu Dias reaches the southern tip of Africa. Portuguese colonies in Africa will soon be created.

1500s – Trading bases
Arab traders establish a base on the island of Zanzibar, Tanzania, East Africa. From here and other bases on the Indian Ocean coast they export African ivory and slaves.

1600s – Slave trade
Beginning of the Atlantic slave trade, first by the Dutch, and in the 18th century by the British. One estimate is that 9 million people crossed the Atlantic to be slaves in the Caribbean and North and South America between 1648 and 1815.

• The TIMELINE continues on page 31.

CITY LIFE IN CAIRO

Cairo's skyscrapers tower over the River Nile.

Life in Cairo, Egypt's capital, is a mixture of modern and ancient. In Cairo cars, taxis and buses share the crowded streets with donkey carts.

Many people make their living from the tourists who come to see the wonders of ancient Egypt.

The lives of affluent people are very similar to those of prosperous people in European cities. For poor people, life is not so very different to how it was centuries ago.

People statistic: *Cairo is the African city with the largest population – 16.5 million people.*

The pyramids, built 2500 BC, stand on the edge of Cairo.

WODAABE COURTSHIP RITUALS

The Wodaabe nomad people of Niger have a unique ritual for finding a marriage partner.

Once a year, the young men dress up and parade in front of the women.

The men try to outshine each other and attract a mate by wearing makeup, pulling strange faces, and performing strenuous dances called *geerewol.*

Lifestyle fact: *each woman chooses the man she finds the most beautiful. She may even agree to marry him!*

A young Wodaabe man paints his face.

THE AMHARA OF ETHIOPIA

A subterranean church carved into the rock at Lalibela.

The Amhara people of the central highlands of Ethiopia adopted Christianity over 1700 years ago.

At Lalibela, in Ethiopia, the Amhara created 12 incredible churches. Each church is carved inside and out directly from the solid rock of the hillside.

Lifestyle fact: *the Amhara eat teff, a grain not grown by any other African people. It is made into big pancakes.*

TOWNSHIP LIFE IN SOUTH AFRICA

In South Africa, black people from all over the country have moved to the cities looking for work. They live in 'townships' – shanty towns on the edges of the cities.

People build their own houses from whatever materials they can find. Many do not have running water, sanitation, or electricity.

Many people are unable to find work, or only have low-paid, temporary jobs.

Culture fact: *township people enjoy a wide range of exciting music. The mix of people from across the country can make a township a poor, yet vibrant, place.*

Children in a Capetown shanty town.

THE TUAREG PEOPLE

The nomad Tuareg people live in the Sahara desert and the dry grasslands south of the Sahara.

In the past the Tuaregs traded across the desert. They carried goods on their camels, but today most goods are transported by lorries!

Tuaregs move from place to place with their herds of camels, sheep and goats to find water and new pasture land.

The Tuareg territory covers parts of five African countries – Libya, Algeria, Mali, Niger and Burkina Faso.

The Tuareg are Muslims, and have a distinctive language with its own alphabet.

People fact: *there are around 3 million Tuareg people.*

A Tuareg nomad

DINKA CATTLE HERDERS

The Dinka people of southern Sudan grow crops and raise herds of animals, especially cattle.

The cattle supply milk, meat and urine which is used as an antiseptic.

At dusk, families and their animals gather around fires made from cow dung. The smoke protects the people from insect bites and ash from the dung fires can be rubbed on the skin to repel insects.

Ash is also used as make-up and even toothpaste.

It is the job of the young Dinka men to care for the cattle, protecting them from predators and raids by other tribes.

Cattle are called to their night-time compounds by the beating of a drum. Cattle recognise the beat played by their owner and respond to the individual 'tune'!

People fact: *cattle are selected for the size of their horns. The cattle represent a Dinka family's wealth.*

The boys often have a favourite animal and make up songs about it.

THE ASHANTI PEOPLE OF GHANA

The Ashanti people live in southern Ghana. Arts and crafts are traditionally very important in their culture.

Craftworkers carve wooden stools with images that reflect the owner's personality, and many people in Ghana are buried in coffins specially carved in shapes personal to their lives, such as musical instruments, or animals if they were a farmer.

Ashanti weavers produce elaborately patterned cloth, called 'kente'.

Culture fact: *a special kind of kente cloth is made which is reserved only for the 'asastehene' – the Ashanti king.*

The weaving of kente is done outdoors. Ashanti weavers use their hands and feet to work the loom.

AFRICA TIMELINE

1869 – Suez canal
The Suez canal, connecting the Mediterranean and Red Seas, opens in Egypt.

1870s – Scramble for Africa
European powers carve up Africa into colonies. Liberia and Abyssinia (Ethiopia) remain independent. European explorers and missionaries are active in Africa.

1948 – Apartheid
The South African government introduces *'apartheid'* (apartness) and denys votes and rights to black people.

1956 – Independence in Africa
Start of the 'decolonisation' of Africa by Britain, France, Belgium. In 1956, Sudan becomes independent from Britain.

In 1975, Portugal grants independence to its African colonies.

1985 – Live Aid
The *'Live Aid'* fundraising concert is held to help people suffering famine in Ethiopia.

1994 – End of apartheid
End of apartheid in South Africa. Black leader Nelson Mandela is elected President after spending 28 years in prison for opposing apartheid. Genocide of 800,000 Tutsi people by Hutus in Rwanda.

1997 – Kofi Annan
Kofi Annan, from Ghana, is appointed Secretary General of the United Nations. In 2001, he wins the Nobel Peace Prize for his work.

2002 – Civil war in Angola
The end of 27 years of civil war in Angola. People who have fled the war begin returning home. The work of clearing landmines and rebuilding the country will take many years.

2005 – Darfur/Aid for Africa
The end of 22 years of civil war in South Sudan, but violence breaks out in the western province of Darfur, with fighting between government forces and rebels.

Leaders of the world's richest countries agree plans to help Africa by cancelling debt, increasing aid, and making trade fairer.

PEOPLE *of* AFRICA

MAASAI CATTLE HERDERS

The Maasai cattle herders live a semi-nomadic life along the Great Rift Valley of southern Kenya and northern Tanzania.

Maasai men are grouped into an 'age-set' with their peers. They remain with this group for all the stages of their lives, doing different work at each stage.

Maasai women care for the children, collect firewood and water, grow vegetables and even build the family's home.

Because it is high in protein, cattle blood, extracted from a vein opened up in a cows neck, is given to people suffering from a variety of ills.

Culture fact: *during ceremonies, the moran (young warriors) perform rhythmic vertical jumping which they can maintain for hours!*

Many Maasai now allow tourists to visit their villages and buy Maasai crafts, such as this distinctive beadwork.

In their late teens to twenties, young men are moran, or warriors. During this stage in their lives, they look after the cattle.

THE SAN

The San, or *'bushmen'*, are the original inhabitants of the Kalahari Desert in southern Africa.

They live in family groups, building huts which are abandoned when the food or water in an area becomes scarce.

The San are skilled hunter-gatherers – they gather fruit, edible roots and tubers and set traps to catch small animals and birds.

San men hunt large animals, such as antelope, using simple bows to fire arrows which carry poison extracted from beetle larvae.

Lifestyle fact: *San arrows can take several days to kill a large animal. The hunter follows his prey's tracks waiting for it to succumb to the poison.*

MBENDJELE

The Mbendjele are one of the many peoples known collectively as 'Pygmies'. They live in the rainforests of central Africa.

Mbendjele groups move camp many times each year. They wrap smoking embers from the fire at their old camp in leaves, and then use the embers to start a fire at the new camp.

Mokodis, strings woven from tree bark and vines, are worn to cure illness. They are also tied around the waist of newborn babies to protect them.

Nature and the forest are important to the Mbendjele, and hunters only kill animals as they are needed for food.

Culture fact: *Gorillas are believed to be reincarnated humans and are never hunted.*

ZULUS

The Zulus celebrate their history as warriors by wearing their ritual costumes.

In the early 1800s the Zulus became the mightiest military force in southern Africa.

Today, around 3 million Zulus live in the countryside of Kwa-Zulu Natal, in South Africa. Many Zulu men are forced to make a living working in coal mines hundreds of miles from

their homes and families.

Believing that bad spirits cause bad luck and illness, Zulus consult *isangomas*, specially-trained healers who diagnose illnesses and the causes of illnesses. The ailment is then treated with traditional Zulu medicines made by an *inyanga*.

People fact: *many Zulu women are skilled in making craft items from beads. If a woman wants a relationship with a man, she may send a subtle message to him through her beaded jewellery.*

AFRICA FACTFILES

Africa

The 'factfiles' take a country by country look at the people of Africa. Each factfile contains: **life expectancy** and **infant mortality** figures (these are an important indicator of quality of life and general health); **ethnic groups**, **religions** and **languages spoken** shown as a percentage of the total population; **literacy rates** which can be used to compare the availability and quality of education from country to country; and the **top five industries** ranked by the amount of money they produce annually.

> • See THE GLOSSARY for the ethnic groups, religions, languages and industries in these FACTFILES.

ALGERIA
Total population: 32,531,853
Life expectancy (total population): 73 years
Infant mortality (per 1000 live births): 31 deaths
Ethnic mix: Arab-Berber 99%; others (including European) 1%
Religions: Sunni Muslim 99%; Christian and Jewish 1%
Languages: Arabic, French, Berber dialects
Literacy rate – male: 78.8% / female: 61%
Industries (top 5): Petroleum; natural gas; light industries; mining; electrical goods

ANGOLA
Total population: 11,190,786
Life expectancy (total population): 37 years
Infant mortality (per 1000 live births): 191 deaths
Ethnic mix: Ovimbundu 37%; Kimbundu 25%; Bakongo 13%; others 25%
Religions: Indigenous beliefs 47%; Roman Catholic 38%; Protestant 15%
Languages: Portuguese; Bantu
Literacy rate – male: 56% / female: 28%
Industries (top 5): Petroleum; diamonds; iron ore; phosphates; feldspar

BENIN
Total population: 7,460,025
Life expectancy (total population): 50.5 years
Infant mortality (per 1000 live births): 85 deaths
Ethnic mix: 42 different African ethnic groups
Religions: Indigenous beliefs 50%; Christian 30%; Muslim 20%
Languages: French; Fon; Yoruba
Literacy rate – male: 56.2% / female: 26.5%
Industries: Textiles; food processing; construction materials; cement

BOTSWANA
Total population: 1,640,115
Life expectancy (total population): 34 years
Infant mortality (per 1000 live births): 54.5 deaths
Ethnic mix: Setswana 79%; Kalanga 11%; white 7%; others 3%;
Religions: Christian 71.6%; others 28.4%
Languages: Setswana; Kalanga
Literacy rate – male: 76.9% / female: 82.4%
Industries (top 5): Diamonds; copper; nickel; salt; soda ash

BURKINA FASO
Total population: 13,925,313
Life expectancy (total population): 44 years
Infant mortality (per 1000 live births): 98 deaths
Ethnic mix: Mossi 40%; others (including Gurunsi, Senufo, Lobi, Bobo, Mande and Fulani) 60%
Religions: Muslim 50%; Indigenous beliefs 40%; Christian 10%
Languages: Moore; Jula; French
Literacy rate – male: 36.9% / female: 16.6%
Industries (top 5): Cotton lint; drinks production; agricultural processing; soap; cigarettes

BURUNDI
Total population: 6,370,609
Life expectancy (total population): 43.5 years
Infant mortality (per 1000 live births): 69 deaths
Ethnic mix: Hutu 85%; Tutsi 14%; Twa (Pygmy) 1%
Religions: Christian 67%; indigenous beliefs 23%; Muslim 10%
Languages: Kirundi; French; Swahili
Literacy rate – male: 58.5% / female: 45.2%
Industries: Consumer goods (blankets, shoes, soap); assembly of imported components; public works construction; food processing

CAMEROON
Total population: 16,380,005
Life expectancy (total population): 48 years
Infant mortality (per 1000 live births): 68 deaths
Ethnic mix: Highlanders 31%; Equatorial Bantu 19%; Kirdi 11%; Fulani 10%; Northwestern Bantu 8%; others 21%
Religions: Indigenous beliefs 40%; Christian 40%; Muslim 20%
Languages: English; French; 24 African languages
Literacy rate – male: 84.7% / female: 73.4%
Industries (top 5): Petroleum; aluminium; food processing; consumer goods; textiles

CAPE VERDE
Total population: 418,224
Life expectancy (total population): 70.5 years
Infant mortality (per 1000 live births): 48 deaths
Ethnic mix: Creole 71%; African 28%; European 1%
Religions: Christianity
Languages: Portuguese; Crioulo
Literacy rate – male: 85.8% / female: 69.2%
Industries (top 5): Food and drinks production; fish processing; footwear and clothing; salt mining; ship repair

CENTRAL AFRICAN REPUBLIC
Total population: 3,799,897
Life expectancy (total population): 41 years
Infant mortality (per 1000 live births): 91 deaths
Ethnic mix: Baya 33%; Banda 27%; Mandjia 13%; Sara 10%; Mboum 7%; others 10%
Religions: Indigenous beliefs 35%; Protestant 25%; Roman Catholic 25%; Muslim 15%
Languages: French; Sangho
Literacy rate – male: 63.3% / female: 39.9%
Industries (top 5): Mining (gold and diamonds); timber; brewing; textiles; footwear

CHAD
Total population: 9,826,419
Life expectancy (total population): 48 years
Infant mortality (per 1000 live births): 94 deaths
Ethnic mix: North and centre 200 groups (including Arabs); in the south, Sara, Moundang, Moussei and Massa
Religions: Muslim 51%; Christian 35%; animist 7%; others 7%
Languages: French; Arabic; Sara; 120 different languages and dialects
Literacy rate – male: 56% / female: 39.3%
Industries (top 5): Oil; cotton textiles; meatpacking; beer brewing; natron (sodium carbonate)

COMOROS
Total population: 671,247
Life expectancy (total population): 62 years
Infant mortality (per 1000 live births): 75 deaths
Ethnic mix: Antalote; Cafre; Makoa; Oimatsaha; Sakalava
Religions: Sunni Muslim 98%; Roman Catholic 2%
Languages: Arabic; French; Shikomoro
Literacy rate – male: 63.6% / female: 49.3%
Industries: Tourism; perfume distillation

CONGO (DEMOCRATIC REPUBLIC OF)
Total population: 60,085,804
Life expectancy (total population): 49 years
Infant mortality (per 1000 live births): 93 deaths
Ethnic mix: Over 200 ethnic groups, majority are Bantu
Religions: Roman Catholic 50%; Protestant 20%; Kimbanguist 10%; Muslim 10%; indigenous beliefs 10%
Languages: French; Lingala; Kingwana; Kikongo; Tshiluba
Literacy rate – male: 76.2% / female: 55.1%
Industries (top 5): Mining (diamonds, copper, zinc); mineral processing; consumer products (food, shoes, cigarettes); cement; ship repair

CONGO (REPUBLIC OF)
Total population: 3,039,126
Life expectancy (total population): 49 years
Infant mortality (per 1000 live births): 92 deaths
Ethnic mix: Kongo 48%; Sangha 20%; M'Bochi 12%; Teke 17%; others (including Europeans) 3%
Religions: Christian 50%; animist 48%; Muslim 2%
Languages: French; Lingala; Monokutuba
Literacy rate – male: 89.6% / female: 78.4%
Industries (top 5): Petroleum extraction; cement; timber; brewing; sugar

COTE D'IVOIRE (IVORY COAST)
Total population: 17,298,040
Life expectancy (total population): 49 years
Infant mortality (per 1000 live births): 91 deaths
Ethnic mix: Akan 42.1%; Voltaiques or Gur 17.6%; Northern Mandes 16.5%; Krous 11%; others 12.8%
Religions: Muslim 40%; indigenous beliefs 35%; Christian 25%
Languages: French; Dioula and 60 native dialects
Literacy rate – male: 57.9% / female: 43.6%
Industries (top 5): Food and drinks production; timber products; oil refining; truck and bus assembly; textiles

DJIBOUTI
Total population: 476,703
Life expectancy (total population): 43 years
Infant mortality (per 1000 live births): 104 deaths
Ethnic mix: Somali 60%; Afar 35%; others (French, Arab, Ethiopian and Italian) 5%
Religions: Muslim 94%; Christian 6%
Languages: French; Arabic; Somali; Afar
Literacy rate – male: 78% / female: 58.4%
Industries: Construction; agricultural processing; salt

AFRICA *Factfiles*

EGYPT
Total population: 77,505,756
Life expectancy (total population): 71 years
Infant mortality (per 1000 live births): 33 deaths
Ethnic mix: Egyptians, Bedouins and Berbers 99%; others 1%
Religions: Sunni Muslim 94%; Christian 6%
Languages: Arabic; English; French
Literacy rate – male: 68.3% / female: 46.9%
Industries (top 5): Textiles; food processing; tourism; chemicals; hydrocarbons

EQUATORIAL GUINEA
Total population: 535,881
Life expectancy (total population): 55.5 years
Infant mortality (per 1000 live births): 85 deaths
Ethnic mix: Bioko; Rio Muni
Religions: Christianity
Languages: Spanish; French
Literacy rate – male: 93.3% / female: 78.4%
Industries: Petroleum; fishing; timber; natural gas

ERITREA
Total population: 4,561,599
Life expectancy (total population): 52 years
Infant mortality (per 1000 live births): 75 deaths
Ethnic mix: Tigrinya 50%; Tigre and Kunama 40%; Afar 4%; others (including Red Sea coast dwellers) 6%
Religions: Muslim; Christian
Languages: Afar; Arabic; Tigre; Kuname; Tigrinya
Literacy rate – male: 69.9% / female: 47.6%
Industries (top 5): Food processing; drinks production; clothing and textiles; salt; cement

ETHIOPIA
Total population: 75,053,286
Life expectancy (total population): 49 years
Infant mortality (per 1000 live births): 95 deaths
Ethnic mix: Oromo 40%; Amhara and Tigre 32%; others 28%
Religions: Muslim 45%; Christian 35%; animist 12%; others 8%
Languages: Amharic; Tigrinya; Oromigna; Guaragigna; Somali; Arabic
Literacy rate – male: 50.3% / female: 35.1%
Industries (top 5): Food processing; drinks production; textiles; chemicals; metal processing

GABON
Total population: 1,389,201
Life expectancy (total population): 56 years
Infant mortality (per 1000 live births): 54 deaths
Ethnic mix: Bantu tribes (including Fang, Bapounou, Nzebi and Obamba); other Africans; Europeans
Religions: Christian; animist
Languages: French; Fang; Myene; Nzebi
Literacy rate – male: 73.7% / female: 53.3%
Industries (top 5): Petroleum extraction and refining; mining (manganese and gold); chemicals; ship repair; food and drinks production

GAMBIA (THE)
Total population: 1,593,256
Life expectancy (total population): 55 years
Infant mortality (per 1000 live births) : 72 deaths
Ethnic mix: Mandinka 42%; Fula 18%; Wolof 16%; Jola 10%; Serahuli 9%; others 5%
Religions: Muslim 90%; Christian 9%; indigenous beliefs 1%
Languages: English; Mandinka; Wolof
Literacy rate – male: 47.8% / female: 32.8%
Industries (top 5): Processing peanuts; fish and hides; tourism; drinks production; agricultural machinery

GHANA
Total population: 21,029,853
Life expectancy (total population): 56 years
Infant mortality (per 1000 live births): 51 deaths
Ethnic mix: Black African (including Akan, Moshi-Dagomba, Ewe, Ga, Gurma and Yoruba tribes) 98.5%; others 1.5%
Religions: Christian 63%; Muslim 16%; indigenous beliefs 21%
Languages: Twi; Fante; Ga; Hausa; Dagbani; English
Literacy rate – male: 82.7% / female: 67.1%
Industries (top 5): Mining; timber; light manufacturing; aluminium smelting; food processing

GUINEA
Total population: 9,467,866
Life expectancy (total population): 50 years
Infant mortality (per 1000 live births): 90 deaths
Ethnic mix: Peuhl 40%; Malinke 30%; Soussou 20%; others 10%
Religions: Muslim 85%; Christian 8%; indigenous beliefs 7%
Languages: French
Literacy rate – male: 49.9% / female: 21.9%
Industries (top 5): Bauxite; gold; diamonds; alumina refining; light manufacturing

GUINEA-BISSAU
Total population: 1,416,027
Life expectancy (total population): 47 years
Infant mortality (per 1000 live births): 107 deaths
Ethnic mix: Balanta 30%; Fula 20%; Manjaca 14%; others 36%
Religions: Indigenous beliefs 50%; Muslim 45%; Christian 5%
Languages: Crioulo; Balante; Pulaar; Mandjak; Mandinka; Portuguese
Literacy rate – male: 58.1% / female: 27.4%
Industries: Processing agricultural products; drinks production

KENYA
Total population: 33,829,590
Life expectancy (total population): 48 years
Infant mortality (per 1000 live births): 61 deaths
Ethnic mix: Kikuyu 22%; Luhya 14%; Luo 13%; Kalenjin 12%; Kamba 11%; others 28%
Religions: Protestant 45%; Roman Catholic 33%; indigenous beliefs 10%; Muslim 10%; others 2%
Languages: Swahili; English; Bantu
Literacy rate – male: 90.6% / female: 79.7%
Industries (top 5): Consumer goods (batteries, soap, cigarettes); agricultural products; oil refining; aluminium; steel

LESOTHO
Total population: 1,867,035
Life expectancy (total population): 37 years
Infant mortality (per 1000 live births): 84 deaths
Ethnic mix: Sotho 99.7%; others (including Europeans and Asians) 0.3%
Religions: Christian 80%; indigenous beliefs 20%
Languages: Sesotho; English; Zulu; Xhosa
Literacy rate – male: 74.5% / female: 94.5%
Industries: Food and drinks production; textiles; handicrafts

LIBERIA
Total population: 3,482,211
Life expectancy (total population): 48 years
Infant mortality (per 1000 live births): 129 deaths
Ethnic mix: Indigenous African tribes 95%; Americo-Liberians 2.5%; Congo people 2.5%
Religions: Indigenous beliefs 40%; Christian 40%; Muslim 20%
Languages: Kpelle; English; Bassa
Literacy rate – male: 73.3% / female: 41.6%
Industries: Rubber processing; palm oil processing; timber; diamonds

LIBYA
Total population: 5,599,053
Life expectancy (total population): 76.5 years
Infant mortality (per 1000 live births): 25 deaths
Ethnic mix: Berber and Arab 97%; others 3%
Religions: Sunni Muslim 97%; others 3%
Languages: Arabic; Italian; English
Literacy rate – male: 92.4% / female: 72%
Industries (top 5): Petroleum; iron and steel; food processing; textiles; handicrafts

MADAGASCAR
Total population: 18,040,341
Life expectancy (total population): 57 years
Infant mortality (per 1000 live births): 77 deaths
Ethnic mix: Malayo-Indonesian; Cotiers; French; Indian; Creole; Comoran
Religions: Indigenous beliefs 52%; Christian 41%; Muslim 7%
Languages: French; Malagasy
Literacy rate – male: 75.5% / female: 62.5%
Industries (top 5): Meat processing; soap; breweries; tanneries; sugar

MALAWI
Total population: 12,158,924
Life expectancy (total population): 37 years
Infant mortality (per 1000 live births): 103 deaths
Ethnic mix: Chewa; Nyanja; Tumbuka; Yao; Lomwe; Sena; Tonga; Ngoni; Ngonde; Asian; European
Religions: Christian 79.9%; Muslim 12.8%; others 7.3%
Languages: Chichewa; Chinyanja; Chiyao; Chitumbuka
Literacy rate – male: 76.1% / female: 49.8%
Industries (top 5): Tobacco; tea; sugar; timber products; cement

MALI
Total population: 12,291,529
Life expectancy (total population): 45 years
Infant mortality (per 1000 live births): 117 deaths
Ethnic mix: Mande 50%; Peul 17%; Voltaic 12%; Songhai 6%; Tuareg and Moor 10%; others 5%
Religions: Muslim 90%; indigenous beliefs 9%; Christian 1%
Languages: Bambara; Fulani; Songhai; French
Literacy rate – male: 53.5% / female: 39.6%
Industries: Food processing; construction; phosphate and gold mining

MAURITANIA
Total population: 3,086,859
Life expectancy (total population): 53 years
Infant mortality (per 1000 live births): 71 deaths
Ethnic mix: Mixed Maur and black 40%; Moor 30%; Black 30%
Religions: Islam
Languages: Arabic; Pulaar; Soninke; French; Hassaniya; Wolof
Literacy rate – male: 51.8% / female: 31.9%
Industries: Fish processing; mining of iron ore and gypsum

MAURITIUS
Total population: 1,230,602
Life expectancy (total population): 72 years
Infant mortality (per 1000 live births): 15 deaths
Ethnic mix: Mauritian 73%; Creole 27%
Religions: Hindu 48%; Christian 32.2%; Muslim 16.6%; others 3.2%
Languages: Creole; Bhojpuri; French
Literacy rate – male: 88.6% / female: 82.7%
Industries (top 5): Sugar milling; textiles; clothing; chemicals; metal products

MAYOTTE
Total population: 193,633
Life expectancy (total population): 61 years
Infant mortality (per 1000 live births): 62 deaths
Ethnic mix: Moharais (from Madagascar)
Religions: Muslim 97%; Christian 3%
Languages: Mahorian; French
Industries: Lobster and shrimp industry; construction

MOROCCO
Total population: 32,725,847
Life expectancy (total population): 71 years
Infant mortality (per 1000 live births): 42 deaths
Ethnic mix: Arab-Berber
Religions: Muslim 98.7%; Christian 1.1%; Jewish 0.2%
Languages: Arabic; Berber dialects; French
Literacy rate – male: 64.1% / female: 39.4%
Industries (top 5): Phosphate rock mining and processing; food processing; leather goods; textiles; construction

MOZAMBIQUE

Total population: 19,406,703
Life expectancy (total population): 40 years
Infant mortality (per 1000 live births): 131 deaths
Ethnic mix: Makhuwa; Tsonga; Lomwe; Sena
Religions: Christian 41.3%; Muslim 17.8%; no religion 23.1%; others 17.8%;
Languages: Emakhuwa; Xichangana; Portuguese
Literacy rate – male: 63.5% / **female:** 32.7%
Industries (top 5): Food and drinks production; chemicals (fertiliser, soap, paints); aluminium; petroleum products; textiles

NAMIBIA

Total population: 2,030,692
Life expectancy (total population): 44 years
Infant mortality (per 1000 live births): 49 deaths
Ethnic mix: Black 87.5% (around 50% belong to the Ovambo tribe); white 6%; mixed 6.5%
Religions: Christian 90%; indigenous beliefs 10%
Languages: English; Afrikaans; German; indigenous languages
Literacy rate – male: 84.4% / **female:** 83.7%
Industries: Meatpacking; fish processing; dairy products; mining (diamond, lead, zinc, tin, silver)

NIGER

Total population: 11,665,937
Life expectancy (total population): 42 years
Infant mortality (per 1000 live births): 122 deaths
Ethnic mix: Hausa 56%; Djerma 22%; Fula 8.5%; Tuareg 8%; Beri Beri 4.3%; others 1.2%
Religions: Muslim 80%; indigenous and Christian 20%
Languages: French; Hausa; Djerma
Literacy rate – male: 25.8% / **female:** 9.7%
Industries (top 5): Uranium mining; cement; bricks; soap; textiles

NIGERIA

Total population: 128,771,988
Life expectancy (total population): 47 years
Infant mortality (per 1000 live births): 99 deaths
Ethnic mix: 250 ethnic groups including Hausa, Yoruba and Igbo
Religions: Muslim 50%; Christian 40%; indigenous beliefs 10%
Languages: Hausa; Yoruba; Igbo; English; Fulani
Literacy rate – male: 75.7% / **female:** 60.6%
Industries (top 5): Crude oil; coal; tin; columbite; palm oil

REUNION

Total population: 776,948
Life expectancy (total population): 74 years
Infant mortality (per 1000 live births): 8 deaths
Ethnic mix: French; African; Malagasy; Chinese; Pakistani; Indian
Religions: Roman Catholic 86%; others (including Hindu, Muslim and Buddhist) 14%
Languages: French; Creole
Literacy rate – male: 87% / **female:** 90.8%
Industries (top 5): Sugar; rum; cigarettes; handicrafts; flower oils

RWANDA

Total population: 8,440,820
Life expectancy (total population): 47 years
Infant mortality (per 1000 live births): 91 deaths
Ethnic mix: Hutu 84%; Tutsi 15%; Twa (Pygmy) 1%
Religions: Roman Catholic 56.5%; Protestant 37.1%; Muslim 4.6%; indigenous beliefs 0.1%; no religion 1.7%
Languages: Kinyarwanda; French; English; Kiswahili
Literacy rate – male: 76.3% / **female:** 64.7%
Industries (top 5): Cement; agricultural products; drinks; soap; furniture

SAO TOME AND PRINCIPE

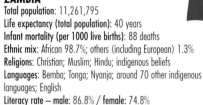

Total population: 187,410
Life expectancy (total population): 67 years
Infant mortality (per 1000 live births): 43 deaths
Ethnic mix: Mestico; Angolares; Forres; Servicais; Tongas; Portuguese
Religions: Catholic 70.3%; others 29.7%
Languages: Portuguese
Literacy rate – male: 85% / **female:** 62%
Industries (top 5): Construction; textiles; soap; beer; fish processing

SENEGAL

Total population: 11,126,832
Life expectancy (total population): 57 years
Infant mortality (per 1000 live births): 55.5 deaths
Ethnic mix: Wolof 43.3%; Pular 23.8%; Serer 14.7%; others 18.2%
Religions: Muslim 94%; Christian 5%; indigenous beliefs 1%
Languages: Wolof; French; Pulaar; Jola; Mandinka
Literacy rate – male: 50% / **female:** 30.7%
Industries (top 5): Food and fish processing; phosphate mining; fertiliser production; petroleum refining; construction materials

SEYCHELLES

Total population: 81,188
Life expectancy (total population): 72 years
Infant mortality (per 1000 live births): 15.5 deaths
Ethnic mix: Mixed descent French, African, Indian, Chinese and Arab
Religions: Roman Catholic 82.3%; Anglican 6.4%; others 11.3%
Languages: Creole; English
Literacy rate – male: 56% / **female:** 60%
Industries (top 5): Fishing; tourism; processing of coconuts and vanilla; coir (coconut fibre) ropes; boat building

SIERRA LEONE

Total population: 6,017,643
Life expectancy (total population): 42.5 years
Infant mortality (per 1000 live births): 144 deaths
Ethnic mix: Temne 30%; Mende 30%; other African tribes 30%; Creole 10%
Religions: Muslim 60%; indigenous beliefs 30%; Christian 10%
Languages: Mende; Temne; Krio; English
Literacy rate – male: 45.4% / **female:** 18.2%
Industries: Diamond mining; small scale manufacturing (textiles, cigarettes, shoes); petroleum refining; ship repair

SOMALIA

Total population: 8,591,629
Life expectancy (total population): 48 years
Infant mortality (per 1000 live births): 117 deaths
Ethnic mix: Somali 85%; others (including Bantu) 15%
Religions: Sunni Muslim
Languages: Somali; Arabic; English
Literacy rate – male: 49.7% / **female:** 25.8%
Industries: Sugar refining; textiles

SOUTH AFRICA

Total population: 44,344,136
Life expectancy (total population): 43 years
Infant mortality (per 1000 live births): 62 deaths
Ethnic mix: Black African 79%; white 9.6%; coloured 8.9%; Asian 2.5%
Religions: Christianity
Languages: IsiZulu; IsiXhosa; Afrikaans; Sepedi; English
Literacy rate – male: 87% / **female:** 85.7%
Industries (top 5): Mining (platinum, gold, chromium); car assembly; metalworking; machinery production; textiles

SUDAN

Total population: 40,187,486
Life expectancy (total population): 58.5 years
Infant mortality (per 1000 live births): 62.5 deaths
Ethnic mix: Black 52%; Arab 39%; Beja 6%; others 3%
Religions: Sunni Muslim 70%; indigenous beliefs 25%; Christian 5%
Languages: Arabic; Nubian; Ta Bedawie; Sudanic languages; English
Literacy rate – male: 71.8% / **female:** 50.5%
Industries (top 5): Oil; cotton processing; textiles; cement; edible oils

SWAZILAND

Total population: 1,173,900
Life expectancy (total population): 36 years
Infant mortality (per 1000 live births): 69 deaths
Ethnic mix: African 97%; European 3%
Religions: Zionist 40%; Roman Catholic 20%; Muslim 10%; others 30%
Languages: English; siSwati
Literacy rate – male: 82.6% / **female:** 80.8%
Industries (top 5): Mining (coal, raw asbestos); wood pulp; sugar; soft drinks concentrates; textiles

TANZANIA

Total population: 36,766,356
Life expectancy (total population): 45 years
Infant mortality (per 1000 live births): 98.5 deaths
Ethnic mix: Bantu (over 130 tribes) 95%; others 5%
Religions: Christian 30%; Muslim 35%; indigenous beliefs 35%; (The Tanzanian island of Zanzibar is 99% Muslim)
Languages: Swahili; Kiunguja; English; Arabic
Literacy rate – male: 85.9% / **female:** 70.7%
Industries: Agricultural processing; mining (diamond, gold, iron); oil refining; footwear

TOGO

Total population: 5,681,519
Life expectancy (total population): 53 years
Infant mortality (per 1000 live births): 67 deaths
Ethnic mix: Black African (37 tribes) 99%; others (including Europeans and Syrian-Lebanese) 1%
Religions: Indigenous beliefs 51%; Christian 29%; Muslim 20%
Languages: Mina; Ewe; Kabye; Dagomba; French
Literacy rate – male: 75.4% / **female:** 46.9%
Industries (top 5): Phosphate mining; agricultural processing; cement; handicrafts; textiles

TUNISIA

Total population: 10,074,951
Life expectancy (total population): 75 years
Infant mortality (per 1000 live births): 25 deaths
Ethnic mix: Arab 98%; others (including European and Jewish) 2%
Religions: Muslim 98%; others (including Christian and Jewish) 2%
Languages: Arabic; French
Literacy rate – male: 84% / **female:** 64.4%
Industries (top 5): Petroleum; mining (phosphate, iron ore); tourism; textiles; footwear

UGANDA

Total population: 27,269,482
Life expectancy (total population): 51.5 years
Infant mortality (per 1000 live births): 68 deaths
Ethnic mix: Baganda 17%; Ankole 8%; Basoga 8%; Iteso 8%; Bakiga 7%; others (including 14 ethnic groups) 52%
Religions: Roman Catholic 33%; Protestant 33%; Muslim 16%; indigenous beliefs 18%
Languages: Luganda; English; Swahili
Literacy rate – male: 79.5% / **female:** 60.4%
Industries (top 5): Sugar; brewing; tobacco; cotton textiles; cement

ZAMBIA

Total population: 11,261,795
Life expectancy (total population): 40 years
Infant mortality (per 1000 live births): 88 deaths
Ethnic mix: African 98.7%; others (including European) 1.3%
Religions: Christian; Muslim; Hindu; indigenous beliefs
Languages: Bemba; Tonga; Nyanja; around 70 other indigenous languages; English
Literacy rate – male: 86.8% / **female:** 74.8%
Industries (top 5): Copper mining and processing; construction; food and drinks production; chemicals; textiles

ZIMBABWE

Total population: 12,746,990
Life expectancy (total population): 37 years
Infant mortality (per 1000 live births): 68 deaths
Ethnic mix: Shona 82%; Ndebele 14%; others 4%
Religions: Syncretic (mixture of different religions) 50%; Christian 25%; indigenous beliefs 24%; others (including Muslim) 1%
Languages: Shona; Ndebele; English;
Literacy rate – male: 94.2% / **female:** 87.2%
Industries (top 5): Mining (many metallic and non-metallic ores); steel; timber; cement; chemicals

TOTAL POPULATION

Total population of Europe:
800,000,000

COUNTRIES BY POPULATION

European countries with highest population:

Russian Federation	143,420,309
Germany	82,431,390
Turkey	69,660,559
France	60,656,178
United Kingdom	60,441,457

Lowest population:

Liechtenstein	33,717
Monaco	32,409
San Marino	28,880
Gibraltar	27,884
Vatican City	921

POPULATION BELOW POVERTY LINE

Moldova	80%
Macedonia	30.2%
Serbia-Montenegro	30%

• See GLOSSARY for a definition of POVERTY LINE.

INTERNET USERS

COUNTRY	INTERNET USERS
Germany	39,000,000
United Kingdom	25,000,000
France	21,900,000
Italy	18,500,000
Spain	9,789,000
Poland	8,970,000

• This list represents the European countries with the highest number of Internet users.

The majority of European people enjoy a good standard of living. Europeans have access to education and healthcare; they have comfortable homes and material possessions; and they have the free time and money to enjoy holidays and visits to theatres, cinemas, restaurants and sporting events. In the past 100 years, people have migrated to Europe from around the world, and today, many large European cities are home to people from many different ethnic groups and cultures.

A Spanish Flamenco dancer in a traditional, colourful dress. Flamenco was developed by Andalucian gypsies, in Spain, 600 years ago. Dancers perform to fast-paced guitar music.

AGE STRUCTURE

MEDIAN AGE is the age that divides a population in two — half the people are younger than this age and half are older.

Median age for Europe

Total population:	38 years
Male:	37 years
Female:	39.5 years

Age structure
These charts show the age structure of the populations of three European countries.

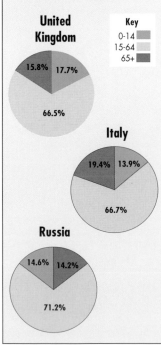

United Kingdom
- 15.8%
- 17.7%
- 66.5%

Key
- 0-14
- 15-64
- 65+

Italy
- 19.4%
- 13.9%
- 66.7%

Russia
- 14.6%
- 14.2%
- 71.2%

STATISTICS: PEOPLE OF EUROPE

Average life expectancy across continent:
Male: 73 years
Female: 80 years

Highest life expectancy:
Andorra 83.5 years

Lowest life expectancy:
Moldova 65 years

Death rate: 10
(average annual number of deaths per 1000 people)

Birth rate: 11
(average annual number of births per 1000 people)

Total fertility rate: 1.5
(average number of children born per woman)

Infant mortality
9 deaths per 1000 live births
(average annual number of deaths of infants under one year old)

ANNUAL INCOME (PER PERSON)

This chart gives an overview of the average annual income per person in 10 European countries. It ranges from the highest income to the lowest. Luxembourg has the world's highest annual income per person in the world.

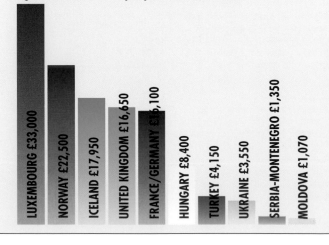

- LUXEMBOURG £33,000
- NORWAY £22,500
- ICELAND £17,950
- UNITED KINGDOM £16,650
- FRANCE/GERMANY £16,100
- HUNGARY £8,400
- TURKEY £4,150
- UKRAINE £3,550
- SERBIA-MONTENEGRO £1,350
- MOLDOVA £1,070

POPULATION GROWTH

Population growth rates per year in some European countries:

Belarus	−0.9%
Germany	0%
Ireland	1.16%
Russia	−0.37%
United Kingdom	0.28%

THE EUROPEAN UNION

The European Union (EU) is an organisation set up to allow European states to band together to support each other.

The EU has set up laws to: help member countries trade easily; allow EU workers to work in any other EU country without permits or visas; and to protect EU workers.

Many people in EU countries are worried that being part of the EU will threaten the culture of their individual country. People called *Euro-sceptics* campaign against their governments signing up to EU laws.

EUROPEAN UNION: TIMELINE

1957 — THE EEC
France, Germany, Italy, Belgium, Luxembourg and the Netherlands sign *The Treaty of Rome* and form the European Economic Community (EEC – later the European Community EC), with the aim of abolishing tariffs and trading restrictions between members.

1973-1986 — NEW MEMBERS
Denmark, Ireland and the United Kingdom (UK) join the EC in 1973; Greece in 1981; Spain and Portugal in 1986.

1992 — THE EUROPEAN UNION
The EC becomes the EU, and, in 1992, *The Maastricht Treaty* prepares the ground for members to work together in areas such as defence, foreign policy and social policies.

1995 — 15 EU MEMBERS
Austria, Finland and Sweden join.

1999 — A NEW CURRENCY
1 January, the Euro is launched as a unit of exchange throughout the EU. Sweden, Denmark and the UK do not join.

2004 - EXPANSION
Ten new countries join the EU, bringing the membership to 25.

• *EU member countries have an EU FLAG in the EUROPE FACTFILES on page 41.*

TOTAL POPULATION OF EUROPEAN UNION

Total population of 25 EU member states:

457,000,000

The European Union (EU) flag has 12 stars for the countries who were members when the EU was named in 1992.

3100-2500 BC — Stonehenge
Neolithic people in England transport massive stones and build the famous stone circle in three phases over 1000 years.

100 AD — Roman Empire
The Roman Empire includes all of western and Mediterranean Europe.

5th century — Invaders
Beginning of barbarian invasions. Roman Empire destroyed. Angles and Saxons from Denmark and north Germany settle in England.

900 — The Vikings
Vikings from Scandinavia raid around the North Sea. They settle in northern England.

1347-51 — Black Death
The Black Death (bubonic plague) kills one third of the people of Europe.

1462 — Russian Empire
Beginning of the expansion of Russia. The Russian Empire will eventually reach from the Baltic and Black Seas to the Pacific Ocean.

1492 — Columbus
Spanish navigator Christopher Columbus discovers the 'New World'. Many European countries will colonise North and South America over the next two centuries.

**1700s-1800s
Industrial Revolution**
The *Industrial Revolution* in Britain starts a period of rapid economic growth, which spreads to many European countries. Populations grow quickly, and people move to the new industrial cities.

1789 — French Revolution
The French Revolution introduces the ideas of *liberty, equality, and fraternity*.

1815 — Battle of Waterloo
The armies of Britain and Prussia (a north German state) defeat the French army led by Napoleon at the Battle of Waterloo.

• The TIMELINE continues on page 39.

PEOPLE *of* EUROPE

SWIMMING IN ICELAND

Iceland is a mass of volcanic rock in the middle of the north Atlantic. It was first settled by people from Norway in the 9th century.

Over 60% of the population live in or around Reykjavik, the capital. Reykjavik means 'Smokey Bay'. It was named for the steam rising from the hot springs, or geysers.

Icelanders do not need to use polluting fuels such as gas, oil or coal to produce their power. The steam from seawater boiled by molten lava, 2 kilometres below the ground, is used by the Svartsengi power station to heat fresh water for homes and to power turbines to produce electricity.

Lifestyle fact: *surrounded by sea and with hot springs and naturally hot outdoor pools, everyone in Iceland goes swimming — even in the winter.*

Bathers enjoy the warm waters of the Blue Lagoon near Reykjavik. Hot water which has been used by the Svartsengi power station flows into the pool.

BULB FARMERS OF THE NETHERLANDS

The Dutch have been growing flower bulbs since the 1500s. The Netherlands, or Holland, are the world's largest producer of bulbs.

Along the northwest coast, in the Northern Sand District, thousands of families make a living growing tulip and daffodil bulbs, on bulb farms.

Most of the farms are located a few kilometres from the sea where the sandy soil is perfect for growing bulbs.

Dutch growers also produce flowers to sell in florist shops and garden plants to sell in garden centres.

People fact: *the farmers sell their cut flowers at large auctions. The flowers are then exported to western Europe, Japan and the USA.*

**This field of tulips will be cut for selling, and then the bulbs dug up and sold to gardeners around the world.
Every year around 3 billion tulip bulbs are grown in Holland.**

THE PEOPLE OF CHERNOBYL

On 26 April, 1986, a nuclear reactor at the Chernobyl Nuclear Power Station in the Ukraine exploded dispersing radioactive particles over parts of the Ukraine, Belarus and western Russia.

Almost 400,000 people have had to leave their homes in the areas contaminated by fallout from Chernobyl.

In Belarus rural families have had to leave their villages to live in high-rise blocks in unfamiliar cities. Many poor families, who rely on home-grown food, are forced to grow vegetables in contaminated soil.

In parts of Belarus, the Ukraine and Russia there has been a significant increase in the number of people suffering from serious illnesses, and an increase in the number of babies born with disabilities.

People fact: *charities around the world have arranged for more than half a million Chernobyl children to have holidays away from the contaminated region.*

A wooden house in Belarus. The people of Belarus are among the poorest in Europe.

MUSLIM COMMUNITY OF PARIS

France has a large number of Muslim migrants from Algeria and Morocco.

In central Paris, the Muslim community is concentrated in the Barbès neighbourhood. Here there are mosques, steam baths, and restaurants serving couscous, the traditional food of North Africa.

Shops and stalls in the Barbès neighbourhood sell the food and cooking equipment of North Africa, copies of the Qu'ran, prayer beads, and prayer mats.

Lifestyle fact: *some people still dress in traditional North African clothes and speak Arabic.*

THE ROMA

The Roma, or gypsies, are travelling people. They migrated from northern India to Europe about 1000 years ago.

Roma gypsies live all over Europe, but their biggest populations are in Romania, Bulgaria and Hungary.

Traditionally, the Roma travelled in horse-drawn caravans and made their living as tinkers and horse-dealers. The Roma of Britain still gather every year at the Appleby Horse Fair in Cumbria, which dates back to the late 1600s.

When Roma die, they are buried with their jewellery, food, tools and even money. After the funeral the rest of their belongings are destroyed, usually by burning.

People statistic: *worldwide, there are more than 12 million Roma.*

MULTICULTURAL LONDON

London has long been a refuge for people fleeing persecution. European Jews came at the end of the 19th century, and again in the 1930s. In recent times, people escaping from conflicts, such as the war in Bosnia, have added to London's mix.

In the 1950s, a wide range of people arrived in London: black people from the West Indies and Africa; Asians from India, Pakistan, and Bangladesh; and Chinese from Hong Kong.

Many West Indian people from the Caribbean settled in Notting Hill where they started an annual Carnival, with decorated floats, extravagant costumes, and the music of their home islands — calypso, steel bands and reggae.

Culture fact: *the Notting Hill Carnival began in 1964. It is now Europe's biggest carnival.*

At the Notting Hill carnival spectators dance and blow whistles as the floats, bands and dancers pass by.

THE VATICAN CITY

The Vatican City is the headquarters of the Roman Catholic church, and the home of the Pope, the leader of the world's one billion Catholics.

Vatican City is the smallest state in the world. It lies in the centre of Rome and has an area of just 109 acres.

Within the Vatican city are the palace of the Pope, St Peter's Basilica, the Sistine Chapel and the Vatican Museums.

The Vatican runs its own railway and radio stations.

People fact: *Vatican city even has its own army — the Swiss Guard.*

The Swiss Guard's colourful uniforms were designed by the artist Michelangelo over 500 years ago.

EUROPE TIMELINE

1847-48 — Potato Famine
With the potato providing the main food source for many in Ireland, successive crop failures lead to the Irish Potato Famine – one million die of starvation, and one million emigrate to Britain and the USA.

1914-1918 — Great War
The First World War: 8.5 million soldiers die.

1917 — Russian Revolution
The Russian Revolution brings a Communist government to power and leads to the formation of the USSR.

1921 — Irish independence
Ireland wins independence from Britain.

1939-1945 — World War II
Second World War: military losses 14.4 million; civilian losses 27.1 million.

1945-1948 — Communism
USSR imposes Communist governments on many East European countries occupied at the end of World War II, including East Germany.

1957 — EEC formed
European Economic Community is formed.

• See THE EUROPEAN UNION page 37

1961 — First man in space
12 April – Russian cosmonaut Yuri Gagarin becomes first man in space.

1966 — World Cup
England hosts and wins the football World Cup.

1989 — German reunification
End of Communist regimes in Russia and Eastern Europe. Communist East Germany and West Germany are reunited.

1992-1995 — Bosnian war
Around 250,000 killed in civil war.

• See page 40 WAR AND PEACE IN BOSNIA

1998 — World Cup
France hosts and wins the football World Cup.

2004 — EU enlarged
European Union enlarged to 25 members.

PEOPLE *of* EUROPE

MEDITERRANEAN FARMERS

On the hot, dry, rocky slopes of hills around the Mediterranean, in countries such as Spain, France, Greece and Italy small farms grow a distinctive range of crops.

Grapes are grown to make wine; olives for olive oil; oranges and lemons; garlic and tomatoes.

People follow the rhythm of the seasons, sowing crops, shearing their sheep, harvesting, and picking grapes.

Every community has its own distinctive culture and festival days. In the town of Bunol in Spain every August thousands of Spanish people and foreign visitors squash over 113,000 kilos of tomatoes — then throw them at each other!

Lifestyle fact: *young people are leaving this hard 'peasant-farmer' way of life for jobs in the cities.*

An Italian farmer in Tuscany harvests grapes
for making Chianti wine

STUTTGART MOTOR CITY

Many cities in Europe owe their prosperity to car factories. Stuttgart in Germany, is the oldest. It is the home of the Mercedes and Porsche factories.

The car factories brought prosperity to Stuttgart; and the promise of prosperity brought workers to the city. Out of Stuttgart's population of 590,000 people 24 per cent are migrant, non-nationals.

Lifestyle fact: *when the car industry is doing well, people will work shifts so the factory is busy 24 hours a day. In bad times, they may lose their jobs.*

WAR AND PEACE IN BOSNIA

Bosnia's history left it with three different communities: Catholic Croats, Eastern Orthodox Serbs, and Muslims.

Between 1918 and 1992, Bosnia was part of Yugoslavia. When Yugoslavia broke up, the Croats in Bosnia wanted to join Croatia, the Serbs wanted to join with Serbia, and the Muslims wanted Bosnia to remain independent.

Merciless civil war broke out in 1992 with all sides carrying out ethnic cleansing: killing or expelling people of the other communities.

Peace came in 1995, but it is fragile. Each community fears and suspects the others.

Bosnia is still a very poor and traumatised country — people grieve for their loved ones, and many are disabled because of their injuries.

People fact: *many Bosnians fled to other European countries for safety. Not all have returned.*

MOUNTAIN PEOPLE OF THE ALPS

The Alps are an enormous chain of mountains running from France, through Switzerland, Liechtenstein and Italy to Austria and Slovenia.

Small communities live in Alpine villages that cling to the mountains and nestle in the valleys

Cattle graze the mountain slopes in the summer, and from their milk distinctive cheeses are made, such as Emmental — the Swiss cheese with the holes!

Other industries in Switzerland include making chocolate, watches, Swiss Army knives and cuckoo clocks!

Communities in the Alps also make a living from tourism. In the winter people come to ski, and in the summer to walk, climb, and sail in the lakes.

People statistic: *in many Alpine villages the tourists outnumber local villagers 40 to 1 during the skiing season.*

An Alpine village. In the distance is the Matterhorn.

EUROPE FACTFILES

Europe

Each country by country factfile contains: **life expectancy** and **infant mortality** figures (important indicators of quality of life and general health); **ethnic groups** and **religions** (shown as a percentage of the population, where figures are available); **main languages spoken** (listed in order of number of speakers); **literacy rates** (which can be used to compare the quality of education from country to country; many European countries have close to 100% literacy so do not publish figures); and the **top five industries** ranked by the amount of money they produce for the country each year.

> • See **THE GLOSSARY** for the ethnic groups, religions, languages and industries in these **FACTFILES**.

ALBANIA

Total population: 3,563,112
Life expectancy (total population): 77 years
Infant mortality (per 1000 live births): 21.5 deaths
Ethnic mix: Albanian 95%; Greek 3%; others 2%
Religions: Muslims 70%; Albanian Orthodox 20%; Roman Catholic 10%
Languages: Albanian; Greek, Vlach
Literacy rate – male: 93.3% / female: 79.5%
Industries (top 5): Food processing; textiles; soap; timber; oil

ANDORRA
Total population: 70,549
Life expectancy (total population): 83.5 years
Infant mortality (per 1000 live births): 4 deaths
Ethnic mix: Spanish 43%; Andorran 33%; Portuguese 11%; French 7%; others 6%
Religions: Roman Catholic
Languages: Catalan; French; Castilian; Portuguese
Industries: Tourism (skiing); cattle farming; timber; banking

AUSTRIA
Total population: 8,184,691
Life expectancy (total population): 79 years
Infant mortality (per 1000 live births): 5 deaths
Ethnic mix: Austrians 91.1%; former Yugoslavs (Croatians, Slovenes, Serbs and Bosnians) 4%; Turks 1.6%; German 0.9%; others 2.4%
Religions: Roman Catholic 73.6%; Protestant 4.7%; Muslim 4.2%; others 5.5%; no religion 12%
Languages: German; Slovene; Croatian; Hungarian
Industries (top 5): Construction; machinery production; vehicles and parts manufacturing; food processing; metals

BELARUS
Total population: 10,300,483
Life expectancy (total population): 69 years
Infant mortality (per 1000 live births): 14 deaths
Ethnic mix: Belarussian 81.2%; Russian 11.4%; Polish 3.9%; Ukrainian 2.4%; others 1.1%
Religions: Eastern Orthodox 80%; others (including Roman Catholic, Protestant, Jewish and Muslim) 20%
Languages: Belarussian; Russian
Literacy rate – male: 99.8% / female: 99.5%
Industries (top 5): Production of metal-cutting machine tools; trucks; tractors and earthmovers; motorcycles; televisions

BELGIUM
Total population: 10,364,388
Life expectancy (total population): 79 years
Infant mortality (per 1000 live births): 5 deaths
Ethnic mix: Flemish 58%; Walloon 31%; others 11%
Religions: Roman Catholic 75%; others (including Protestant) 25%
Languages: Dutch; French; German
Industries (top 5): Engineering and metal products; motor vehicle assembly; transport equipment; scientific instrument production; food and drink processing

BOSNIA–HERZEGOVINA

Total population: 4,025,476
Life expectancy (total population): 73 years
Infant mortality (per 1000 live births): 21 deaths
Ethnic mix: Bosniak 48%; Serbs 37.1%; Croats 14.3%; others 0.6%
Religions: Muslim 40%; Orthodox 31%; Roman Catholic 15%; others 14%
Languages: Bosnian; Croatian; Serbian
Industries (top 5): Steel; coal; iron ore; lead; zinc

BULGARIA
Total population: 7,450,349
Life expectancy (total population): 72 years
Infant mortality (per 1000 live births): 21 deaths
Ethnic mix: Bulgarian 83.9%; Turk 9.4%; Roma 4.7%; others 2%
Religions: Bulgarian Orthodox 82.6%; Muslim 12.2%; others 5.2%
Languages: Bulgarian; Turkish; Roma
Literacy rate – male: 99.1% / female: 98.2%
Industries (top 5): Electricity production; gas and water; food and drinks production; tobacco; machinery production

CROATIA

Total population: 4,495,904
Life expectancy (total population): 74 years
Infant mortality (per 1000 live births): 7 deaths
Ethnic mix: Croat 89.6%; Serb 4.5%; others 5.9%
Religions: Roman Catholic 87.8%; other Christian 4.8%; Muslim 1.3%; others 0.9%; no religion 5.2%
Languages: Croatian; Serbian
Literacy rate – male: 99.4% / female: 97.8%
Industries (top 5): Chemicals and plastics; machine tools; fabricated metal; electronics; pig iron and rolled steel products

CYPRUS

Total population: 780,133
Life expectancy (total population): 78 years
Infant mortality (per 1000 live births): 7 deaths
Ethnic mix: Greek 77%; Turkish 18%; others 5%
Religions: Greek Orthodox 78%; Muslim 18%; others 4%
Languages: Greek; Turkish; English
Literacy rate – male: 98.9% / female: 96.3%
Industries (top 5): Tourism; food and drink processing; cement and gypsum production; ship repairs; textiles

CZECH REPUBLIC

Total population: 10,241,138
Life expectancy (total population): 76 years
Infant mortality (per 1000 live births): 4 deaths
Ethnic mix: Czech 90.4%; Moravian 3.7%; Slovak 1.9%; others 4%
Religions: Roman Catholic 26.8%; Protestant 2.1%; others 3.3%; unspecified 8.8%; unaffiliated 59%
Languages: Czech
Industries (top 5): Metallurgy; machinery and equipment manufacture; motor vehicle manufacture; glass; armaments

DENMARK

Total population: 5,432,335
Life expectancy (total population): 78 years
Infant mortality (per 1000 live births): 5 deaths
Ethnic mix: Scandinavian; Inuit; Faroese; German; Turkish; Iranian
Religions: Christian 98%; Muslim 2%
Languages: Danish; Faroese; Greenlandic; German
Industries (top 5): Metals (including iron and steel); chemicals; food processing; machinery and transport equipment; textiles

ESTONIA
Total population: 1,332,893
Life expectancy (total population): 72 years
Infant mortality (per 1000 live births): 8 deaths
Ethnic mix: Estonian 67.9%; Russian 25.6%; Ukrainian 2.1%; Belarussian 1.3%; Finn 0.9%; others 2.2%
Religions: Evangelical Lutheran; Russian and Estonian Orthodox
Languages: Estonian; Russian
Industries (top 5): Engineering; electronics; timber and timber products; textiles; information technology

FAROE ISLANDS
Total population: 49,962
Life expectancy (total population): 80 years
Infant mortality (per 1000 live births): 6 deaths
Ethnic mix: Scandinavian
Religions: Evangelical Lutheran
Languages: Faroese (derived from old Norse); Danish
Industries: Fishing; fish processing; shipyards; handicrafts

FINLAND

Total population: 5,223,442
Life expectancy (total population): 79 years
Infant mortality (per 1000 live births): 4 deaths
Ethnic mix: Finn 93.4%; Swedish 5.7%; Russian 0.4%; Estonian 0.2%; Roma 0.2%; Sami 0.1%
Religions: Lutheran National Church 84.2%; Greek Orthodox in Finland 1.1%; other Christian 1.1%; others 0.1%; no religion 13.5%
Languages: Finnish; Swedish
Industries (top 5): Metals and metal products; electronics; machinery and scientific equipment manufacture; shipbuilding; pulp and paper

FRANCE

Total population: 60,656,178
Life expectancy (total population): 80 years
Infant mortality (per 1000 live births): 4 deaths
Ethnic mix: Celtic and Latin with Teutonic; Slavic; North African; Indochinese; Basque minorities
Religions: Roman Catholic 85%; Protestant 2%; Jewish 1%; Muslim 8%; unaffiliated 4%
Languages: French
Industries (top 5): Machinery; chemicals; car manufacture; metallurgy; aircraft manufacture

EUROPE *Factfiles*

GERMANY
Total population: 82,431,390
Life expectancy (total population): 79 years
Infant mortality (per 1000 live births): 4 deaths
Ethnic mix: German 91.5%; Turkish 2.4%; others 6.1%
Religions: Roman Catholic 34%; Protestant 34%; Muslim 3.7%; others 28.3%
Languages: German
Industries (top 5): Production of iron and steel; coal; cement; chemicals; machinery, vehicles and machine tools.

GIBRALTAR
Total population: 27,884
Life expectancy (total population): 80 years
Infant mortality (per 1000 live births): 5 deaths
Ethnic mix: Spanish; Italian; English; Maltese; Portuguese; German; North African
Religions: Roman Catholic 78.1%; Protestant 10.2%; Muslim 4%; Jewish 2.1%; Hindu 1.8%; others 3.8%
Languages: English; Spanish; Italian; Portuguese
Industries: Tourism; banking and finance; ship repair; tobacco

GREECE
Total population: 10,668,354
Life expectancy (total population): 79 years
Infant mortality (per 1000 live births): 5.5 deaths
Ethnic mix: Greek 98%; others 2%
Religions: Greek Orthodox 98%; Muslim 1.3%; others 0.7%
Languages: Greek
Literacy rate – male: 98.6% / **female:** 96.5%
Industries (top 5): Tourism; food and tobacco processing; textiles; chemicals; metal products

GUERNSEY
Total population: 65,228
Life expectancy (total population): 80 years
Infant mortality (per 1000 live births): 5 deaths
Ethnic mix: British and French descent
Religions: Christianity
Languages: English; French
Industries: Tourism and banking

HUNGARY
Total population: 10,006,835
Life expectancy (total population): 72 years
Infant mortality (per 1000 live births): 8.5 deaths
Ethnic mix: Hungarian 92.3%; Roma 1.9%; others 5.8%
Religions: Roman Catholic 54.5%; Protestant 19.9%; others (including unaffiliated) 25.6%
Languages: Hungarian
Literacy rate – male: 99.5% / **female:** 99.3%
Industries (top 5): Mining; metallurgy; construction materials; processed foods; textiles

ICELAND
Total population: 296,737
Life expectancy (total population): 80 years
Infant mortality (per 1000 live births): 3 deaths
Ethnic mix: Mix of Norse and Celtic descendants 94%; others 6%
Religions: Lutheran Church of Iceland 85.5%; other Christian 8.3%; others (including unaffiliated) 6.2%
Languages: Icelandic; English
Industries (top 5): Fishing and fish processing; aluminium smelting; ferrosilicon production; geothermal power; tourism

IRELAND

Total population: 4,015,676
Life expectancy (total population): 77.5 years
Infant mortality (per 1000 live births): 5 deaths
Ethnic mix: Celtic; English
Religions: Roman Catholic 88.4%; Church of Ireland 3%; other Christian 1.6%; others 7%
Languages: English; Irish (Gaelic/Gaeilge)
Industries (top 5): Steel; lead; zinc; silver; aluminium

ISLE OF MAN

Total population: 75,049
Life expectancy (total population): 78 years
Infant mortality (per 1000 live births): 6 deaths
Ethnic mix: Manx (Norse-Celtic descent); British
Religions: Christianity
Languages: English; Manx Gaelic
Industries: Financial services; light manufacturing; tourism

ITALY

Total population: 58,103,033
Life expectancy (total population): 80 years
Infant mortality (per 1000 live births): 6 deaths
Ethnic mix: Italian; small numbers of mixed Italian–German/French/Slovene/Albanian/Greek
Religions: Roman Catholic
Languages: Italian
Literacy rate – male: 99% / **female:** 98.3%
Industries (top 5): Tourism; machinery production; iron and steel; chemicals; food processing

JERSEY

Total population: 90,812
Life expectancy (total population): 79 years
Infant mortality (per 1000 live births): 5 deaths
Ethnic mix: Jersey 51.1%; British 34.8%; others (including Irish, French, Portuguese and Madeiran) 14.1%
Religions: Christianity
Languages: English
Industries: Tourism; banking and finance; dairy

LATVIA
Total population: 2,290,237
Life expectancy (total population): 71 years
Infant mortality (per 1000 live births): 9.5 deaths
Ethnic mix: Latvian 57.7%; Russian 29.6%; Belarussian 4.1%; Ukrainian 2.7%; Polish 2.5%; Lithuanian 1.4%; others 2%
Religions: Lutheran; Roman Catholic; Russian Orthodox
Languages: Latvian; Russian
Industries (top 5): Production of buses, vans, cars and railway carriages; synthetic fibres; agricultural machinery; fertilisers; washing machines

LIECHTENSTEIN
Total population: 33,717
Life expectancy (total population): 80 years
Infant mortality (per 1000 live births): 5 deaths
Ethnic mix: Alemannic 86%; others (including Italian and Turkish) 14%
Religions: Roman Catholic 76.2%; Protestant 7%; others 16.8%
Languages: German
Industries (top 5): Electronics; metal manufacturing; dental products; ceramics; pharmaceuticals

LITHUANIA

Total population: 3,596,617
Life expectancy (total population): 74 years
Infant mortality (per 1000 live births): 7 deaths
Ethnic mix: Lithuanian 83.4%; Polish 6.7%; Russian 6.3%; others 3.6%
Religions: Roman Catholic 79%; Russian Orthodox 4.1%; Protestant 1.9%; no religion 9.5%; others 5.5%
Languages: Lithuanian; Russian
Literacy rate – male: 99.7% / **female:** 99.6%
Industries (top 5): Production of metal-cutting tools; electric motors; television sets; refrigerators and freezers; petroleum refining

LUXEMBOURG
Total population: 468,571
Life expectancy (total population): 79 years
Infant mortality (per 1000 live births): 5 deaths
Ethnic mix: Celtic (with French/German); Portuguese; Italian; Slavs (from Montenegro, Albania and Kosovo); other Europeans
Religions: Roman Catholic 87%; others (including Protestant, Jewish and Muslim) 13%
Languages: Luxembourgish; German; French
Industries (top 5): Banking; iron and steel; food processing; chemicals; metal products

MACEDONIA

Total population: 2,045,262
Life expectancy (total population): 74 years
Infant mortality (per 1000 live births): 10 deaths
Ethnic mix: Macedonian 64.2%; Albanian 25.2%; Turkish 3.9%; Roma 2.7%; Serb 1.8%; others 2.2%
Religions: Macedonian Orthodox; Muslim
Languages: Macedonian; Albanian
Industries (top 5): Coal; metallic chromium, lead, zinc and ferronickel; textiles; timber products; tobacco

MALTA

Total population: 398,534
Life expectancy (total population): 79 years
Infant mortality (per 1000 live births): 4 deaths
Ethnic mix: Maltese
Religions: Roman Catholic
Languages: Maltese; English
Literacy rate – male: 92% / **female:** 93.6%
Industries (top 5): Tourism; electronics; ship building and repair; construction; food and drinks production

MOLDOVA

Total population: 4,455,421
Life expectancy (total population): 65 years
Infant mortality (per 1000 live births): 40 deaths
Ethnic mix: Moldovan/Romanian 64.5%; Ukrainian 13.8%; Russian 13%; others 8.7%
Religions: Eastern Orthodox 98%; Jewish 1.5%; others 0.5%
Languages: Moldovan; Russian; Gagauz (a Turkish dialect)
Literacy rate – male: 99.6% / **female:** 98.7%
Industries (top 5): Food processing; agricultural machinery; foundry equipment; refrigerators and freezers; washing machines

MONACO
Total population: 32,409
Life expectancy (total population): 79.5 years
Infant mortality (per 1000 live births): 5 deaths
Ethnic mix: French 47%; Monegasque 16%; Italian 16%; others 21%
Religions: Roman Catholic
Languages: French; English; Italian; Monegasque
Industries: Tourism; construction; small-scale industrial and consumer products

NETHERLANDS

Total population: 16,407,491
Life expectancy (total population): 79 years
Infant mortality (per 1000 live births): 5 deaths
Ethnic mix: Dutch 83%; others (including Turks, Moroccans, Antilleans, Surinamese and Indonesians) 17%
Religions: No religion 41%; Roman Catholic 31%; Dutch reformed 13%; Calvinist 7%; Muslim 5.5%; others 2.5%
Languages: Dutch; Frisian
Industries (top 5): Agro-industries; metal and engineering products; electrical machinery and equipment; chemicals; petroleum

NORWAY

Total population: 4,593,041
Life expectancy (total population): 80 years
Infant mortality (per 1000 live births): 4 deaths
Ethnic mix: Norwegian; Sami (approx 20,000 people)
Religions: Church of Norway 85.7%; other Christian 4.4%; Muslim 1.8%; others 8.1%
Languages: Bokmal Norwegian; Nynorsk Norwegian; small Sami and Finnish-speaking minorities
Industries (top 5): Petroleum and gas; food processing; shipbuilding; pulp and paper products; metals

POLAND

Total population: 38,635,144
Life expectancy (total population): 74 years
Infant mortality (per 1000 live births): 8.5 deaths
Ethnic mix: Polish 96.7%; German 0.4%; Belarussian 0.1%; Ukrainian 0.1%, others 2.7%
Religions: Roman Catholic 89.8%, Eastern Orthodox 1.3%; Protestant 0.3%; others 8.6%
Languages: Polish
Literacy rate – male: 99.8% / female: 99.7%
Industries (top 5): Machine building; iron and steel; coal mining; chemicals; shipbuilding

PORTUGAL

Total population: 10,566,212
Life expectancy (total population): 77.5 years
Infant mortality (per 1000 live births): 5 deaths
Ethnic mix: Mediterranean peoples
Religions: Roman Catholic 94%; Protestant 6%
Languages: Portuguese; Mirandese
Literacy rate – male: 95.5% / female: 91.3%
Industries (top 5): Textiles and footwear; wood pulp, paper and cork; metals and metalworking; oil refining; chemicals

ROMANIA

Total population: 22,329,977
Life expectancy (total population): 71 years
Infant mortality (per 1000 live births): 26 deaths
Ethnic mix: Romanian 89.5%; Hungarian 6.6%; Roma 2.5%; Ukrainian 0.3%; German 0.3%; Russian 0.2%; Turkish 0.2%; others 0.4%
Religions: Eastern Orthodox 86.8%; Protestant 7.5%; Roman Catholic 4.7%; others (including Muslim) 1%
Languages: Romanian; Hungarian; German
Literacy rate – male: 99.1% / female: 97.7%
Industries (top 5): Textiles and footwear; light machinery and car assembly; mining; timber; construction materials

RUSSIAN FEDERATION

Total population: 143,420,309
Life expectancy (total population): 67 years
Infant mortality (per 1000 live births): 15 deaths
Ethnic mix: Russian 79.8%; Tatar 3.8%; Ukrainian 2%; Bashkir 1.2%; Chuvash 1.1%; others 12.1%
Religions: Russian Orthodox; Muslim
Languages: Russian
Literacy rate – male: 99.7% / female: 99.5%
Industries (top 5): Mining and extraction industries (including coal, oil, gas); machine building (including aircraft and space vehicles); defence industries; shipbuilding; transportation equipment

SAN MARINO

Total population: 28,880
Life expectancy (total population): 82 years
Infant mortality (per 1000 live births): 6 deaths
Ethnic mix: Sammarinese; Italian
Religions: Roman Catholic
Languages: Italian
Literacy rate – male: 97% / female: 95%
Industries (top 5): Tourism; banking; textiles; electronics; ceramics

SERBIA-MONTENEGRO

Total population: 10,829,175
Life expectancy (total population): 75 years
Infant mortality (per 1000 live births): 13 deaths
Ethnic mix: Serb 62.6%; Albanian 16.5%; Montenegrin 5%; Hungarian 3.3%; others 12.6%
Religions: Orthodox 65%; Muslim 19%; Roman Catholic 4%; Protestant 1%; others 11%
Languages: Serbian; Albanian
Literacy rate – male: 97.2% / female: 88.9%
Industries (top 5): Machine building (including aircraft, trucks, agricultural machinery and weapons); metallurgy; mining; consumer goods; electronics

SLOVAKIA

Total population: 5,431,363
Life expectancy (total population): 74.5 years
Infant mortality (per 1000 live births): 7 deaths
Ethnic mix: Slovak 85.8%; Hungarian 9.7%; Roma 1.7%; others 2.8%
Religions: Roman Catholic 68.9%; no religion 13%; Protestant 10.8%; Greek Catholic 4.1%; others 3.2%
Languages: Slovak; Hungarian
Industries (top 5): metal and metal products; food and drinks production; fuels (electricity, gas, coke, oil, nuclear fuel); chemicals and man-made fibres; machinery

SLOVENIA

Total population: 2,011,070
Life expectancy (total population): 76 years
Infant mortality (per 1000 live births): 4 deaths
Ethnic mix: Slovene 83.1%; Serb 2%; Croat 1.8%; Bosniak 1.1%; others 12%
Religions: Roman Catholic 57.8%; no religion 10.1%; Orthodox 2.3%; other Christian 0.9%; Muslim 2.4%; others 26.5%
Languages: Slovenian; Serbo-Croatian
Industries (top 5): Metal products; lead and zinc smelting; electronics (including military); trucks; electric power equipment

SPAIN

Total population: 40,341,462
Life expectancy (total population): 79.5 years
Infant mortality (per 1000 live births): 4 deaths
Ethnic mix: Mediterranean
Religions: Roman Catholic 94%; others 6%
Languages: Castilian Spanish; Catalan; Galician; Basque
Literacy rate – male: 98.7% / female: 97.2%
Industries (top 5): Textiles and footwear; food and drinks production; metals and metal products; chemicals; shipbuilding

SWEDEN

Total population: 9,001,774
Life expectancy (total population): 80 years
Infant mortality (per 1000 live births): 3 deaths
Ethnic mix: Swedes; Finns; Sami
Religions: Lutheran 87%; others (including Roman Catholic, Orthodox, Baptist, Muslim, Jewish and Buddhist) 13%
Languages: Swedish; small Sami and Finnish-speaking minorities
Industries (top 5): Iron and steel; precision equipment (radio and telephone parts, armaments); wood pulp and paper products; food processing; vehicle manufacture

SWITZERLAND

Total population: 7,489,370
Life expectancy (total population): 80 years
Infant mortality (per 1000 live births): 4 deaths
Ethnic mix: German 65%; French 18%; Italian 10%; others 7%
Religions: Roman Catholic 41.8%; Protestant 37.5%; no religion 11.1%; Muslim 4.3%; others 5.3%
Languages: German; French; Italian
Industries (top 5): Machinery; chemicals; watches; textiles; precision instruments

TURKEY

Total population: 69,660,559
Life expectancy (total population): 72 years
Infant mortality (per 1000 live births): 41 deaths
Ethnic mix: Turkish 80%; Kurdish 20%
Religions: Islam
Languages: Turkish; Kurdish; Arabic; Armenian; Greek
Literacy rate – male: 94.3% / female: 78.7%
Industries (top 5): Textiles; food processing; vehicle manufacture; mining (coal, chromite, copper, boron); steel

UKRAINE

Total population: 47,425,336
Life expectancy (total population): 67 years
Infant mortality (per 1000 live births): 20 deaths
Ethnic mix: Ukrainian 77.8%; Russian 17.3%; others 4.9%
Religions: Ukrainian Orthodox 44%; Ukrainian Greek Catholic 6%; Ukrainian Autocephalous Orthodox 1.7%; others (including no religion) 48.3%
Languages: Ukrainian; Russian
Industries (top 5): Coal; electric power; metals; machinery and transport equipment; chemicals

UNITED KINGDOM

Total population: 60,441,457
Life expectancy (total population): 78 years
Infant mortality (per 1000 live births): 5 deaths
Ethnic mix: white 92.1%; black 2%; Indian 1.8%; Pakistani 1.3%; others 2.8%
Religions: Christian 71.6%; Muslim 2.7%; Hindu 1%; others (including no religion) 24.7%
Languages: English
Industries (top 5): Machine tools; electric power equipment; automation equipment; railroad equipment; shipbuilding

VATICAN CITY

Total population: 921
Ethnic mix: Italians; Swiss
Religions: Roman Catholic
Languages: Italian; Latin

The Sami people live in Lapland – a vast, snowy wilderness stretching across northern Scandinavia and Russia. Many Sami still live a traditional life as reindeer herders.

The peoples of Asia are extremely diverse with many different lifestyles and cultures. They also live in extremes of wealth and poverty. The citizens of the wealthy manufacturing nations, such as Singapore and Japan, and oil-rich countries, such as Saudi Arabia, live in modern apartments in gleaming skyscrapers. While in India, thousands live on the streets and do not have enough to eat.

Farmers take a break from planting in Rajasthan, India. Millions of people across Asia work in centuries old industries such as fishing, raising animals and growing rice.

TOTAL POPULATION

Total population of Asia:
3,840,000,000

COUNTRIES BY POPULATION

Asian countries with highest population:

China	1,306,313,812
India	1,080,264,388
Indonesia	241,973,879
Pakistan	162,419,946
Bangladesh	144,319,628

Lowest population:

Qatar	863,051
Bahrain	453,237
Macau	449,198
Brunei	372,361
Maldives	349,106

POPULATION GROWTH

Population growth rates per year in Asia:

Cambodia	1.81%
China	0.58%
Gaza	3.77%
India	1.4%
Uzbekistan	1.67%

INTERNET USERS

COUNTRY	INTERNET USERS
China	94,000,000
Japan	57,200,000
South Korea	29,220,000
India	18,481,000
Taiwan	13,800,000
Malaysia	8,692,100
Indonesia	8,000,000
Thailand	6,971,500
Iran	4,300,000
Philippines	3,500,000

- This list represents the Asian countries with the highest number of Internet users.

STATISTICS: PEOPLE OF ASIA

Average life expectancy across continent:

Male:	67 years
Female:	72 years

Highest life expectancy:
Macau   82 years

Lowest life expectancy:
Afghanistan   43 years

Death rate: 7
(average annual number of deaths per 1000 people)

Birth rate: 23
(average annual number of births per 1000 people)

Total fertility rate: 3
(average number of children born per woman)

Infant mortality:
39 deaths per 1000 live births
(number of deaths of infants under one year old per year):

ANNUAL INCOME (PER PERSON)

This chart gives an overview of the average annual income per person in 10 Asian countries. It ranges from the highest income to the lowest.

- HONG KONG £19,200
- JAPAN £16,500
- SAUDI ARABIA £6,750
- CHINA £3,150
- IRAQ £1,970
- INDIA £1,740
- KYRGYZSTAN £950
- AFGHANISTAN £450
- GAZA STRIP £337
- EAST TIMOR £225

AGE STRUCTURE

MEDIAN AGE is the age that divides a population in two – half the people are younger than this age and half are older.

Median age for Asia

Total population:	26 years
Male:	26 years
Female:	26 years

Age structure
These charts show the age structure of the populations of four Asian countries.

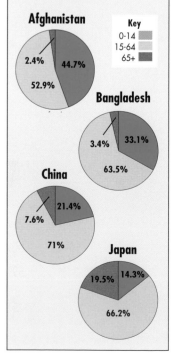

Afghanistan
Key
0-14
15-64
65+
2.4%
44.7%
52.9%

Bangladesh
3.4%
33.1%
63.5%

China
7.6%
21.4%
71%

Japan
19.5%
14.3%
66.2%

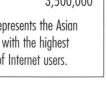

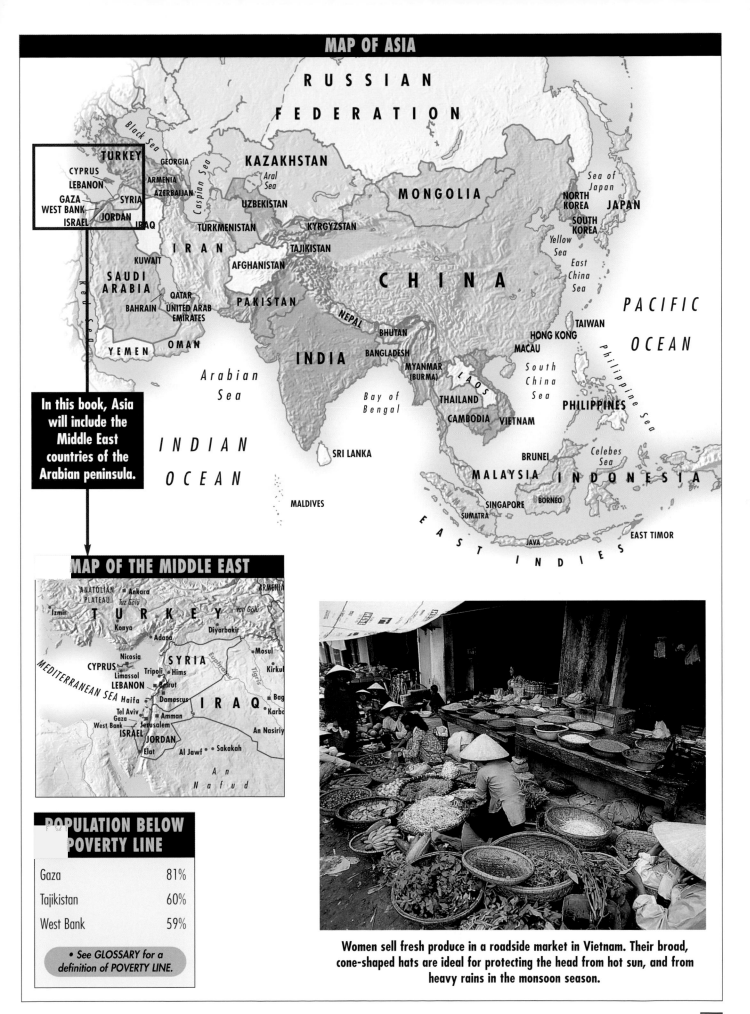

RUSSIAN FEDERATION

KAZAKHSTAN

TURKEY

CYPRUS
LEBANON
GAZA
WEST BANK
ISRAEL
JORDAN
SYRIA
IRAQ

GEORGIA
ARMENIA
AZERBAIJAN

Black Sea

MONGOLIA

Sea of Japan

NORTH KOREA

JAPAN

SOUTH KOREA

Caspian Sea

Aral Sea

UZBEKISTAN

KYRGYZSTAN

Yellow Sea

TURKMENISTAN

IRAN

TAJIKISTAN

AFGHANISTAN

CHINA

East China Sea

KUWAIT

SAUDI ARABIA

QATAR
BAHRAIN

UNITED ARAB EMIRATES

PAKISTAN

NEPAL

BHUTAN

PACIFIC OCEAN

TAIWAN

HONG KONG
MACAU

Red Sea

YEMEN

OMAN

INDIA

BANGLADESH

MYANMAR (BURMA)

South China Sea

Philippine Sea

Arabian Sea

Bay of Bengal

LAOS

THAILAND

PHILIPPINES

In this book, Asia will include the Middle East countries of the Arabian peninsula.

INDIAN OCEAN

SRI LANKA

CAMBODIA

VIETNAM

BRUNEI

Celebes Sea

MALDIVES

MALAYSIA

INDONESIA

SINGAPORE

BORNEO

SUMATRA

JAVA

EAST INDIES

EAST TIMOR

MAP OF THE MIDDLE EAST

ANATOLIAN PLATEAU

Ankara

Tuz Gölü

Van Gölü

ARMENIA

Izmir

TURKEY

Konya

Adana

Diyarbakir

Mosul

SYRIA

Kirkuk

MEDITERRANEAN SEA

CYPRUS

Nicosia

Limassol

Tripoli

Hims

Euphrates

Tigris

LEBANON

Beirut

Haifa

Damascus

Bag

IRAQ

Tel Aviv

Amman

Karba

Gaza

Jerusalem

West Bank

ISRAEL

JORDAN

An Nasiriy

Elat

Al Jawf

Sakakah

An Nafud

POPULATION BELOW POVERTY LINE

Gaza	81%
Tajikistan	60%
West Bank	59%

• See GLOSSARY for a definition of POVERTY LINE.

Women sell fresh produce in a roadside market in Vietnam. Their broad, cone-shaped hats are ideal for protecting the head from hot sun, and from heavy rains in the monsoon season.

• The TIMELINE continues on page 47

BEDOUINS

Bedouins are nomadic Arabs. They originated in the Arabian Peninsula where they used their knowledge of the deserts to act as paid guides, controlling ancient trade routes.

Today, Bedouins live in Saudi Arabia, Egypt, Israel and Jordan.

Many Bedouins are camel breeders.

When Bedouins meet a stranger in the desert, the stranger is given the best food and drink, and becomes an honoured guest.

Bedouin women tend the flocks, cook the meals and even pitch and dismantle the tents. Bedouin tents are in two sections with the front reserved for men and the back for women.

Culture fact: *camels are known as 'God's gift' as they are so well adapted to desert life.*

NENET REINDEER HERDERS

The Nenet reindeer herders live in western Siberia. Some Nenet groups live on the Yamal Peninsular (Yamal means '*the end of the Earth*') where winter temperatures can drop as low as −50℃.

The Nenet people live alongside their animals taking great care of them.

The reindeer provide meat, fur for clothing and hides which are used for making tents. They also pull the Nenet's sleighs.

Nenet people eat some bread and fish, but their staple food is reindeer meat, which is sometimes eaten raw.

Culture fact: *religious idols and other special items are carried on a sacred sleigh which is only unpacked on special occasions by a respected Nenet elder.*

A young Nenet boy wears clothes and boots made from reindeer fur.

MONGOLIAN HORSE PEOPLE

The Mongolian horse people are nomadic livestock farmers who breed horses, yaks, sheep, goats, cattle and camels.

They primarily eat foods made from meat, milk or flour — plant-based foods are considered animal feed!

Their small, stocky horses are a much loved and important part of Mongolian culture. The horses are bred for milk and transport.

Every July, the Mongolian horse people enjoy the three-day *Naadam* festival of horse-racing, archery, wrestling and feasting.

During Naadam, child jockeys, aged between four and ten, race their family's horses.

People statistic: *there are around 600,000 Mongolian horse people.*

Young Mongolian boys tend their family's sheep in the Ovorkhangai Province of Mongolia.

THE SHERPAS OF NEPAL

The Sherpa people live in Tibet, Bhutan, India and Nepal. The largest Nepalese community lives in the Khumbu valley – *'the gateway to Mount Everest'*.

The Sherpa people live their lives at high altitudes and are used to the mountainous terrain and thin air.

They have become famous for acting as guides for people who come to the Himalayas to climb Mount Everest, the world's tallest mountain.

Before climbing Everest, the *puja* ceremony is performed to ask the mountain gods for a safe return.

People fact: *the name 'Sherpa' comes from the Tibetan words for people (shar) and east (wa) – the 'People from the East'.*

In the mountains of Nepal there are no roads so all goods have to be carried.

BUDDHIST MONKS IN THAILAND

Thai Buddhist monks usually start as novices at around 12 years old. All male Thai Buddhists spend some time living as monks.

A Buddhist monk's day begins early with meditation and blessings. Later, the monks bless people in the local community and give them spiritual guidance.

In return, the local community provide food for the monks and everyday needs such as cleaning materials and clothing.

During the *Phansa* period, monks hardly venture out of the monastery and they take special vows. The local community begins Phansa with a candlelit procession to the monastery.

Culture fact: *Phansa began when Buddhist leaders were concerned that their monks would tread on farmers' rice fields during the three-month rainy season. They kept the monks in the monastery to stop them spoiling the crops.*

A young Buddhist monk sits by a huge Buddha statue. Monks shave their heads once a month on the day before the full moon.

UZBEK CULTURE AND TRADITIONS

When Uzbekistan was created by the Soviet Union in the 20th century, a national Uzbek identity emerged.

In the communist era, under the Soviet Union, the nation was officially atheist. Since independence in 1991, Islam has enjoyed renewed support. For many Uzbeks being Muslim is more cultural than religious.

Uzbek men meet to drink green tea with bread at *chai khanas* (tea gardens). They sit on flat wooden beds, and the tea and bread are served in the middle.

The round loaves of bread, known as *nan*, must not be placed upside down and must be torn, rather than cut with a knife.

People fact: *there are Uzbek communities in other Asian countries such as Kazakhstan, China and Afghanistan.*

INDIAN DANCE

Dance is both an art and a way of telling stories in India. Its roots lie in Hinduism.

The god, Shiva, is also *Nataraj – the Lord of the Dance*. Nataraj created *Tandava*, which is the male form of dance, and *Lasya*, the female form.

Each hand, arm, foot, leg, head and eye movement has meaning. Together, they can tell a story.

Culture fact: *the 'Kathakali' form of dance from Kerala in southwest India is danced by men. It tells stories of battles between gods and demons.*

ASIA TIMELINE

1600s — Trade in Asia
Dutch traders discover new trading partners in Asia. *Dutch East India Company* trades in Asian ports.

1700s-1800s — India
The British trade in India through the *British East India Company*. Eventually Britain takes control of India.

1941 — World War II
Japan destroys the US fleet in Pearl Harbor, on island of Hawaii. USA declares war on Japan which leads to Japan uniting with Germany and Italy against Britain, the USA and other Allies. The war is fought on many fronts in Asia, such as Burma.

1947 — Indian Independence
India gains independence from Britain, but is divided into Hindu India and Muslim East and West Pakistan. East Pakistan will become Bangladesh in 1971.

• See page 9
WAR AND PERSECUTION

1948 to present day
Conflict between Israelis and Palestinians – many agreements made and broken.

1949 — Communism in China
Communists gain control in China and form the *People's Republic of China*.

1950-1953 — Korean War
North Korea invades South Korea. The USA joins the war on the side of the South.

1965-1973 — Vietnam war
USA fight with South Vietnam against Communist North Vietnam.

1980s — Technology boom
An electronics and technology boom in Asia is led by Japan.

2004 — Tsunami disaster
On the morning of 26 December, a giant tsunami hits countries with coasts bordering the Indian Ocean, such as Thailand and Sri Lanka. Economies, towns and villages are devastated. The death toll cannot be accurately calculated, but more than 200,000 people are killed.

PEOPLE *of* ASIA

THE MIAO PEOPLE

The Miao people live in a mountainous region of southwest China. With one of the world's most ancient cultures, the 7 million Miao people can trace their ancestors back over 4000 years.

Women's headdresses have great importance in Miao culture.

Each clan has a different design of headdress which is worn at festivals. Adorned with silver ornaments the women dance in the headdresses to show off their family's wealth.

The clan from the village Longga are known as the Long-Horned Miao. The women wear headdresses created by wrapping their hair, and hair from their ancestors, around animal horns.

Culture fact: *Miao girls learn batik and embroidery from an early age. A girl's skill with fabric greatly increases her value as a wife.*

A Long-Horned Miao family.

SRI LANKAN RICE FARMERS

Rice is a major crop for Sri Lanka. Farming communities all help each other to grow the crop.

Before growing rice, the paddy fields are blessed.

The fields are weeded, then the land is ploughed — still using buffalo ploughs in some areas. People pound with their feet to level off the soil, then a flat board is pulled across the field to smooth it out. Seed is then sown.

Children sing and yell in the fields to chase birds off the rice crop as it grows.

Culture fact: *at the 'Alut Sahala Mangallaya' rice ceremony, farmers take rice to the temple and gather it together in one huge bowl to be blessed, and as an offering of thanks.*

KOREAN HANOKS

Traditional stone and wood houses in Korea are called 'hanok'.

A good place to build a house will have a mountain behind and a river in front.

Some houses today still have *'ondol gudeul'*, an ancient system of underfloor warm-air heating, and *'Daechong'*, cool porches with wooden floors for the hot summers.

Lifestyle fact: *rooms in a hanok have no special function — low dining tables or sleeping mats are placed in the room as needed.*

LIFE IN KYOTO, JAPAN

Kyoto is an ancient, religious, cultural and craft centre. It is also a modern, commercial city.

Every day the residents of Kyoto attend the city's 2000 Buddhist temples and Shinto shrines.

Kyoto has many peaceful parks and public gardens. Some parks have over 1000 cherry blossom trees.

Culture fact: *in spring, Japanese people celebrate the time of year with 'hanami': cherry-blossom viewing parties and picnics which are held under the cherry trees.*

- See GLOSSARY for a definition of GEISHA.

Geishas stroll under cherry blossom in a Kyoto garden.

ASIA FACTFILES

Asia

Each country by country factfile contains: **life expectancy** and **infant mortality** figures (important indicators of quality of life and general health); **ethnic groups** and **religions** (shown as a percentage of the population, where figures are available); **main languages spoken** (listed in order of number of speakers); **literacy rates** (which, where available, can be used to compare the quality of education from country to country); and the **top five industries** ranked by the amount of money they produce each year.

AFGHANISTAN

Total population: 29,928,987
Life expectancy (total population): 43 years
Infant mortality (per 1000 live births): 163 deaths
Ethnic mix: Pashtun 42%; Tajik 27%; Uzbek 9%; others 22%
Religions: Muslim 99%; others 1%
Languages: Afghan Persian or Dari; Pashtu
Literacy rate – male: 51% / female: 21%
Industries (top 5): Small-scale production of textiles, soap, furniture, footwear, fertiliser and cement; handwoven carpets; gas; coal; copper

ARMENIA
Total population: 2,982,904
Life expectancy (total population): 71.5 years
Infant mortality (per 1000 live births): 23 deaths
Ethnic mix: Armenian 97.9%; Yezidi (Kurd) 1.3%; others 0.8%
Religions: Christian 98.7%; Yezidi 1.3%
Languages: Armenian; Yezidi
Literacy rate – male: 99.4% / female: 98%
Industries (top 5): Diamond-processing; production of metal-cutting and forging machines; electric motors; tyres; knitted textiles

AZERBAIJAN

Total population: 7,911,974
Life expectancy (total population): 63 years
Infant mortality (per 1000 live births): 82 deaths
Ethnic mix: Azeri 90.6%; Dagestani 2.2%; Russian 1.8%; others 5.4%
Religions: Muslim 93.4%; Jewish 4.8%; others 1.8%
Languages: Azerbaijani; Russian; Armenian
Literacy rate – male: 99% / female: 96%
Industries (top 5): Petrol; gas; petrol products; oilfield equipment; steel

BAHRAIN
Total population: 453,237
Life expectancy (total population): 74 years
Infant mortality (per 1000 live births): 17 deaths
Ethnic mix: Bahraini 62.4%; others 37.6%
Religions: Muslim 81.2%; Christian 9%; others 9.8%
Languages: Arabic; English; Farsi; Urdu
Literacy rate – male: 91.9% / female: 85%
Industries (top 5): Petrol processing and refining; aluminium smelting; iron pelletization; fertilisers; offshore banking

BANGLADESH
Total population: 144,319,628
Life expectancy (total population): 62 years
Infant mortality (per 1000 live births): 63 deaths
Ethnic mix: Bengali 98%; others 2%
Religions: Muslim 83%; Hindu 16%; others 1%
Languages: Bangla (or Bengali); English
Literacy rate – male: 53.9% / female: 31.8%
Industries (top 5): Cotton textiles; jute; clothing; tea processing; paper

BHUTAN

Total population: 2,232,291
Life expectancy (total population): 54 years
Infant mortality (per 1000 live births): 100 deaths
Ethnic mix: Bhote 50%; Nepalese 35%; indigenous tribes 15%
Religions: Buddhist 75%; Hindu 25%
Languages: Dzongkha; Tibetan and Nepalese dialects
Literacy rate – male: 56.2% / female: 28.1%
Industries (top 5): Cement; timber products; processed fruits; alcoholic drinks; calcium carbide

BRUNEI

Total population: 372,361
Life expectancy (total population): 75 years
Infant mortality (per 1000 live births): 13 deaths
Ethnic mix: Malay 67%; Chinese 15%; others 18%
Religions: Muslim 67%; Buddhist 13%; Christian 10%; others (including indigenous beliefs) 10%
Languages: Malay; English; Chinese
Literacy rate – male: 96.3% / female: 91.4%
Industries: Petrol and petrol refining; liquefied natural gas; construction

CAMBODIA
Total population: 13,607,069
Life expectancy (total population): 59 years
Infant mortality (per 1000 live births): 71 deaths
Ethnic mix: Khmer 90%; Vietnamese 5%; Chinese 1%; others 4%
Religions: Buddhist 95%; others 5%
Languages: Khmer; French; English
Literacy rate – male: 80.8% / female: 59.3%
Industries (top 5): Tourism; clothing; rice milling; fishing; timber and timber products

CHINA
Total population: 1,306,313,812
Life expectancy (total population): 72 years
Infant mortality (per 1000 live births): 24 deaths
Ethnic mix: Han Chinese 91.9%; others (including Zhuang, Uygur, Hui, Yi, Tibetan, Miao, Manchu, Mongol, Buyi and Korean) 8.1%
Religions: Officially atheist; Buddhist and Muslim up to 2%; Christian up to 4%
Languages: Mandarin Chinese
Literacy rate – male: 95.1% / female: 86.5%
Industries (top 5): Mining and ore processing (iron, steel, aluminium and other metals); coal; machine building; armaments; textiles

EAST TIMOR
Total population: 1,040,880
Life expectancy (total population): 66 years
Infant mortality (per 1000 live births): 47 deaths
Ethnic mix: Austronesian (Malayo/Polynesian); Papuan
Religions: Roman Catholic 90%; Muslim 4%; Protestant 3%; Hindu 0.5%; others (including Buddhist and animist) 2.5%
Languages: Tetum; Portuguese; Indonesian; English
Literacy rate (total population): 58.6%
Industries: Printing; soap manufacturing; handicrafts; textiles

GAZA STRIP
Total population: 1,376,289
Life expectancy (total population): 72 years
Infant mortality (per 1000 live births): 23 deaths
Ethnic mix: Palestinian Arab
Religions: Islam; Christianity
Languages: Arabic
Industries: Primarily small family-run businesses producing textiles, soap, olive-wood carvings and mother-of-pearl souvenirs

GEORGIA

Total population: 4,677,401
Life expectancy (total population): 76 years
Infant mortality (per 1000 live births): 19 deaths
Ethnic mix: Georgian 83.8%; Azeri 6.5%; Armenian 5.7%; Russian 1.5%; others 2.5%
Religions: Christian 88.6%; Muslim 9.9%; others 1.5%
Languages: Georgian 71%; Russian 9%; Armenian 7%; others 13%
Literacy rate – male: 100% / female: 98%
Industries (top 5): Steel; aircraft production; machine tools; electrical appliances; mining (manganese and copper)

HONG KONG

Total population: 6,898,686
Life expectancy (total population): 81 years
Infant mortality (per 1000 live births): 3 deaths
Ethnic mix: Chinese 95%; others 5%
Religions: Mixture of local religions 90%; Christian 10%
Languages: Chinese; English
Literacy rate – male: 96.9% / female: 89.6%
Industries (top 5): Textiles and clothing; tourism; banking; shipping; electronics

INDIA

Total population: 1,080,264,388
Life expectancy (total population): 64 years
Infant mortality (per 1000 live births): 56 deaths
Ethnic mix: Indo-Aryan 72%; Dravidian 25%; others 3%
Religions: Hindu 80.5%; Muslim 13.4%; Christian 2.3%; Sikh 1.9%; others 1.9%
Languages: English; Hindi; Bengali; Telugu; Marathi; Tamil; Urdu; Gujarati
Literacy rate – male: 70.2% / female: 48.3%
Industries (top 5): Textiles; chemicals; food processing; steel; transport equipment

INDONESIA
Total population: 241,973,879
Life expectancy (total population): 69.5 years
Infant mortality (per 1000 live births): 36 deaths
Ethnic mix: Javanese 45%; Sundanese 14%; Madurese 7.5%; coastal Malays 7.5%; others 26%
Religions: Muslim 88%; Christian 8%; Hindu 2%; Buddhist 1%; others 1%
Languages: Bahasa Indonesia; English; Dutch; Javanese
Literacy rate – male: 92.5% / female: 83.4%
Industries (top 5): Petrol; natural gas; textiles and clothing; footwear; mining

IRAN
Total population: 68,017,860
Life expectancy (total population): 70 years
Infant mortality (per 1000 live births): 42 deaths
Ethnic mix: Persian 51%; Azeri 24%; Gilaki and Mazandarani 8%; Kurd 7%; Arab 3%; others 7%
Religions: Muslim 98%; others (including Zoroastrian, Jewish, Christian and Baha'i) 2%
Languages: Persian; Turkic; Kurdish
Literacy rate – male: 85.6% / female: 73%
Industries (top 5): Petrol; petrochemicals; textiles; cement and other construction materials; sugar refining and vegetable oil production

• See THE GLOSSARY for the ethnic groups, religions, languages and industries in these FACTFILES.

ASIA *Factfiles*

IRAQ

Total population: 26,074,906
Life expectancy (total population): 69 years
Infant mortality (per 1000 live births): 50 deaths
Ethnic mix: Arab 80%; Kurdish 15%; others 5%
Religions: Muslim 97%; others 3%
Languages: Arabic; Kurdish; Assyrian; Armenian
Literacy rate – male: 55.9% / **female:** 24.4%
Industries (top 5): Petrol; chemicals; textiles; construction materials; food processing

ISRAEL

Total population: 6,276,883
Life expectancy (total population): 79 years
Infant mortality (per 1000 live births): 7 deaths
Ethnic mix: Jewish 80.1% (includes people born in Europe, America, Israel, Africa and Asia); Arab 19.9%
Religions: Jewish 76.5%; Muslim 15.9%; Christian 2.1%; others 5.5%
Languages: Hebrew; Arabic; English
Literacy rate – male: 97.3% / **female:** 93.6%
Industries (top 5): High-tech projects (aviation, communications, medical electronics); timber and paper products; potash and phosphates; food and drinks production; tobacco

JAPAN
Total population: 127,417,244
Life expectancy (total population): 81 years
Infant mortality (per 1000 live births): 3 deaths
Ethnic mix: Japanese 99%; others (including Korean, Chinese, Brazilian and Filipino) 1%
Religions: Shinto and Buddhist 84%; others 16%
Languages: Japanese
Literacy rate (total population): 99%
Industries (top 5): Cars; electronic equipment; machine tools; steel and other metals; ships

JORDAN
Total population: 5,759,732
Life expectancy (total population): 78 years
Infant mortality (per 1000 live births): 17 deaths
Ethnic mix: Arab 98%; Circassian 1%; Armenian 1%
Religions: Muslim 92%; Christian 6%; others 2%
Languages: Arabic; English
Literacy rate – male: 95.9% / **female:** 86.3%
Industries (top 5): Phosphate mining; pharmaceuticals; petrol refining; cement; potash

KAZAKHSTAN
Total population: 15,185,844
Life expectancy (total population): 66.5 years
Infant mortality (per 1000 live births): 29 deaths
Ethnic mix: Kazakh 53.4%; Russian 30%; Uzbek 2.5%; others 14.1%
Religions: Muslim 47%; Russian Orthodox 44%; others 9%
Languages: Kazakh; Russian
Literacy rate – male: 99.1% / **female:** 97.7%
Industries (top 5): Oil; coal; iron ore; manganese; chromite

KUWAIT
Total population: 1,044,294
Life expectancy (total population): 77 years
Infant mortality (per 1000 live births): 10 deaths
Ethnic mix: Kuwaiti 45%; other Arab 35%; others 20%
Religions: Muslim 85%; others (including Christian, Hindu and Parsi) 15%
Languages: Arabic; English
Literacy rate – male: 85.1% / **female:** 81.7%
Industries (top 5): Petrol; petrochemicals; cement; shipbuilding and repair; desalination

KYRGYZSTAN

Total population: 5,146,281
Life expectancy (total population): 68 years
Infant mortality (per 1000 live births): 36 deaths
Ethnic mix: Kyrgyz 64.9%; Uzbek 13.8%; Russian 12.5%; others 8.8%
Religions: Muslim 75%; Russian Orthodox 20%; others 5%
Languages: Kyrgyz; Russian
Literacy rate – male: 99% / **female:** 96%
Industries (top 5): Small machinery production; textiles; food processing; cement; footwear

LAOS
Total population: 6,217,141
Life expectancy (total population): 55 years
Infant mortality (per 1000 live births): 85 deaths
Ethnic mix: Lao Loum 68%; Lao Theung 22%; others (including Lao Soung, Hmong and the Yao) 10%
Religions: Buddhist 60%; animist 40%
Languages: Lao; French; English
Literacy rate – male: 77.4% / **female:** 55.5%
Industries (top 5): Mining (tin, gypsum); timber products; electric power; agricultural processing; construction

LEBANON

Total population: 3,826,018
Life expectancy (total population): 73 years
Infant mortality (per 1000 live births): 24.5 deaths
Ethnic mix: Arab 95%; Armenian 4%; others 1%
Religions: Muslim 59.7%; Christian 39%; others 1.3%
Languages: Arabic; French; English; Armenian
Literacy rate – male: 93.1% / **female:** 82.2%
Industries (top 5): Banking; food processing; jewellery; cement; textiles

MACAU
Total population: 449,198
Life expectancy (total population): 82 years
Infant mortality (per 1000 live births): 4 deaths
Ethnic mix: Chinese 95.7%; others 4.3%
Religions: Buddhist 50%; Roman Catholic 15%; others (including no religion) 35%
Languages: Chinese (Cantonese)
Literacy rate – male: 97.2% / **female:** 92%
Industries (top 5): Tourism; gambling; clothing; textiles; electronics

MALAYSIA

Total population: 23,953,136
Life expectancy (total population): 72 years
Infant mortality (per 1000 live births): 18 deaths
Ethnic mix: Malay 50.4%; Chinese 23.7%; Bhumiputera 11%; Indian 7.1%; others 7.8%
Religions: Islam; Buddhism; Taoism; Hinduism; Christianity; Sikhism; Shamanism
Languages: Bahasa Melayu; English; Chinese dialects; Tamil
Literacy rate – male: 92% / **female:** 85.4%
Industries (top 5): Rubber and oil palm processing and manufacturing; light manufacturing; electronics; tin mining and smelting; timber

MALDIVES

Total population: 349,106
Life expectancy (total population): 64 years
Infant mortality (per 1000 live births): 56.5 deaths
Ethnic mix: South Indians; Sinhalese; Arabs
Religions: Muslim (Sunni)
Languages: Maldivian Dhivehi; English is spoken by government officials
Literacy rate – male: 97.1% / **female:** 97.3%
Industries (top 5): Fish processing; tourism; shipping; boat building; coconut processing

MONGOLIA

Total population: 2,791,272
Life expectancy (total population): 64.5 years
Infant mortality (per 1000 live births): 54 deaths
Ethnic mix: Mongol 94.9%; others 5.1%
Religions: Buddhist-Lamaist 50%; no religion 40%; Christian 6%; Muslim 4%
Languages: Khalkha Mongol; Turkic; Russian
Literacy rate – male: 98% / **female:** 97.5%
Industries (top 5): Construction and construction materials; mining; oil; food and drinks production; cashmere and natural fibres

MYANMAR (BURMA)

Total population: 42,909,464
Life expectancy (total population): 56 years
Infant mortality (per 1000 live births): 67 deaths
Ethnic mix: Burman 68%; Shan 9%; Karen 7%; others 16%
Religions: Buddhist 89%; Christian 4%; Muslim 4%; others 3%
Languages: Burmese
Literacy rate – male: 89.2% / **female:** 81.4%
Industries (top 5): Agricultural processing; clothing; timber and timber products; copper; tin

NEPAL
Total population: 27,676,547
Life expectancy (total population): 60 years
Infant mortality (per 1000 live births): 67 deaths
Ethnic mix: Chhettri 15.5%; Brahman-Hill 12.5%; Magar 7%; Tharu 6.6%; Tamang 5.5%; Newar 5.4%; others 47.5%
Religions: Hindu 80.6%; Buddhist 10.7%; others 8.7%
Languages: Nepali; Maithali
Literacy rate – male: 62.7% / **female:** 27.6%
Industries (top 5): Tourism; carpets; textiles; rice; jute

NORTH KOREA
Total population: 22,912,177
Life expectancy (total population): 71 years
Infant mortality (per 1000 live births): 24 deaths
Ethnic mix: Korean; small Chinese and Japanese communities
Religions: Buddhist; Confucianist
Languages: Korean
Literacy rate (total population): 99%
Industries (top 5): Military products; machine building; electric power; chemicals; mining

OMAN
Total population: 2,424,290
Life expectancy (total population): 73 years
Infant mortality (per 1000 live births): 19.5 deaths
Ethnic mix: Arab; Baluchi; Indian; Pakistani; Sri Lankan; Bangladeshi; African
Religions: Muslim 75%; others (including Hindu) 25%
Languages: Arabic; English; Baluchi; Urdu; Indian dialects
Literacy rate – male: 83.1% / **female:** 67.2%
Industries (top 5): Crude oil production and refining; gas production; construction; cement; copper

PAKISTAN
Total population: 162,419,946
Life expectancy (total population): 63 years
Infant mortality (per 1000 live births): 72 deaths
Ethnic mix: Punjabi; Sindhi; Pashtun; Baloch; Muhajir
Religions: Muslim 97%; others (including Christian and Hindu) 3%
Languages: Punjabi; Sindhi; Siraiki; Pashtu; Urdu
Literacy rate – male: 59.8% / **female:** 30.6%
Industries (top 5): Textiles and clothing; food processing; pharmaceuticals; construction materials; paper products

PHILIPPINES

Total population: 87,857,473
Life expectancy (total population): 70 years
Infant mortality (per 1000 live births): 23.5 deaths
Ethnic mix: Tagalog 28.1%; Cebuano 13.1%; Ilocano 9%; Bisaya/Binisaya 7.6%; Hiligaynon Ilonggo 7.5%; others 34.7%
Religions: Roman Catholic 80.9%; others (including Christian, Muslim and indigenous beliefs) 19.1%
Languages: Filipino; English; Tagalog; Cebuano
Literacy rate – male: 92.5% / female: 92.7%
Industries (top 5): Electronics assembly; clothing; footwear; pharmaceuticals; chemicals

QATAR

Total population: 863,051
Life expectancy (total population): 74 years
Infant mortality (per 1000 live births): 19 deaths
Ethnic mix: Arab 40%; Pakistani 18%; Indian 18%; Iranian 10%; others 14%
Religions: Islam
Languages: Arabic; English
Literacy rate – male: 81.4% / female: 85%
Industries (top 5): Crude oil production and refining; ammonia; fertilisers; petrochemicals; steel reinforcing bars

SAUDI ARABIA

Total population: 20,841,523
Life expectancy (total population): 75 years
Infant mortality (per 1000 live births): 13 deaths
Ethnic mix: Arab 90%; Afro-Asian 10%
Religions: Islam
Languages: Arabic
Literacy rate – male: 84.7% / female: 70.8%
Industries (top 5): Crude oil production; petrol refining; petrochemicals; ammonia; industrial gases

SINGAPORE

Total population: 4,425,720
Life expectancy (total population): 82 years
Infant mortality (per 1000 live births): 2 deaths
Ethnic mix: Chinese 76.8%; Malay 13.9%; Indian 7.9%; others 1.4%
Religions: Buddhist 42.5%; Muslim 14.9%; Christian 14.6%; Taoist 8.5%; Hindu 4%; no religion 14.8%; others 0.7%
Languages: Chinese (Mandarin); English; Malay
Literacy rate – male: 96.6% / female: 88.6%
Industries (top 5): Electronics; chemicals; financial services; oil drilling equipment; petrol refining

SOUTH KOREA

Total population: 48,422,644
Life expectancy (total population): 76 years
Infant mortality (per 1000 live births): 7 deaths
Ethnic mix: Korean
Religions: Christian 26%; Buddhist 26%; Confucianist 1%; no religion 46%; others 1%
Languages: Korean
Literacy rate – male: 99.2% / female: 96.6%
Industries (top 5): Electronics; telecommunications; car production; chemicals; shipbuilding

SRI LANKA

Total population: 20,064,776
Life expectancy (total population): 73 years
Infant mortality (per 1000 live births): 14 deaths
Ethnic mix: Sinhalese 73.8%; Sri Lankan Moors 7.2%; Indian Tamil 4.6%; Sri Lankan Tamil 3.9%; others 10.5%
Religions: Buddhist 69.1%; Muslim 7.6%; Hindu 7.1%; others 16.2%
Languages: Sinhala; Tamil; English
Literacy rate – male: 94.8% / female: 90%
Industries (top 5): Rubber processing; tea; coconuts; telecommunications; insurance

SYRIA

Total population: 18,448,752
Life expectancy (total population): 70 years
Infant mortality (per 1000 live births): 29.5 deaths
Ethnic mix: Arab 90.3%; others (including Kurds and Armenians) 9.7%
Religions: Muslim 90%; Christian 10%
Languages: Arabic; Kurdish
Literacy rate – male: 89.7% / female: 64%
Industries (top 5): Petrol; textiles; food processing; drinks production; tobacco

TAIWAN

Total population: 22,894,384
Life expectancy (total population): 77 years
Infant mortality (per 1000 live births): 6 deaths
Ethnic mix: Taiwanese 84%; mainland Chinese 14%; others 2%
Religions: Mixture of Buddhist, Confucian and Taoist 93%; Christian 4.5%; others 2.5%
Languages: Chinese (Mandarin); Taiwanese
Literacy rate (total population): 96.1%
Industries (top 5): Electronics; petrol refining; armaments; chemicals; textiles

TAJIKISTAN

Total population: 7,163,506
Life expectancy (total population): 64.5 years
Infant mortality (per 1000 live births): 111 deaths
Ethnic mix: Tajik 79.9%; Uzbek 15.3%; Russian 1.1%; others 3.7%
Religions: Muslim 90%; others 10%
Languages: Tajik; Russian
Literacy rate – male: 99.6% / female: 99.1%
Industries (top 5): Aluminium, zinc and lead; chemicals and fertilisers; cement; vegetable oil; metal-cutting machine tools

THAILAND

Total population: 65,444,371
Life expectancy (total population): 71.5 years
Infant mortality (per 1000 live births): 20 deaths
Ethnic mix: Thai 75%; Chinese 14%; others 11%
Religions: Buddhist 94.6%; Muslim 4.6%; others 0.8%
Languages: Thai; English
Literacy rate – male: 94.9% / female: 90.5%
Industries (top 5): Tourism; textiles and clothing; agricultural processing; drinks production; tobacco

TURKMENISTAN

Total population: 4,952,081
Life expectancy (total population): 61 years
Infant mortality (per 1000 live births): 73 deaths
Ethnic mix: Turkmen 85%; Uzbek 5%; Russian 4%; others 6%
Religions: Muslim 89%; Eastern Orthodox 9%; others 2%
Languages: Turkmen; Russian; Uzbek
Literacy rate – male: 99% / female: 97%
Industries (top 5): Natural gas; oil; petrol products; textiles; food processing

UNITED ARAB EMIRATES

Total population: 957,133
Life expectancy (total population): 75 years
Infant mortality (per 1000 live births): 14.5 deaths
Ethnic mix: Emirati 19%; other Arab and Iranian 23%; South Asian 50%; others (including Westerners and East Asians) 8%
Religions: Muslim 96%; others 4%
Languages: Arabic; Persian; English; Hindi; Urdu
Literacy rate – male: 76.1% / female: 81.7%
Industries (top 5): Petrol; fishing; aluminium; cement; fertilisers

UZBEKISTAN

Total population: 26,851,195
Life expectancy (total population): 64 years
Infant mortality (per 1000 live births): 71 deaths
Ethnic mix: Uzbek 80%; Russian 5.5%; Tajik 5%; Kazakh 3%; Karakalpak 2.5%; Tatar 1.5%; others 2.5%
Religions: Muslim 88%; Eastern Orthodox 9%; others 3%
Languages: Uzbek; Russian; Tajik
Literacy rate – male: 99.6% / female: 99%
Industries (top 5): Textiles; food processing; machine building; metallurgy; petrol

VIETNAM

Total population: 83,535,576
Life expectancy (total population): 71 years
Infant mortality (per 1000 live births): 26 deaths
Ethnic mix: Kinh (Vietnamese) 86.2%; others 13.8%
Religions: No religion 80.8%; Buddhist 9.3%; others 9.9%
Languages: Vietnamese; English; French; Chinese; Khmer
Literacy rate – male: 93.9% / female: 86.9%
Industries (top 5): Food processing; clothing; footwear; machine building; mining

WEST BANK

Total population: 2,385,615
Life expectancy (total population): 73 years
Infant mortality (per 1000 live births): 20 deaths
Ethnic mix: Palestinian Arab 83%; Jewish 17%
Religions: Muslim 75%; Jewish 17%; Christian and others 8%
Languages: Arabic; Hebrew; English
Industries (top 5): Small family businesses producing cement, textiles, soap, olive-wood carvings and mother-of-pearl souvenirs

YEMEN

Total population: 20,727,063
Life expectancy (total population): 62 years
Infant mortality (per 1000 live births): 61.5 deaths
Ethnic mix: Arab
Religions: Islam
Languages: Arabic
Literacy rate – male: 70.5% / female: 30%
Industries (top 5): Crude oil production; petrol refining; small-scale production of cotton textiles and leather goods; food processing; handicrafts

A Kathakali dancer in India. Special eyedrops are used to make the eyes red, and the face is made up to look like a mask.

50,000 years ago
Pre-historic peoples cross a land bridge on the Torres Strait to colonise Australia and become the first Australians. They bring plants and animals with them to their new world.

10,000 years ago
The Ice Age retreats causing ice melt. Land bridges across Oceania are swamped cutting off migration routes between islands and land masses.

3000 BC — First islanders
South East Asians sail in huge outrigger canoes as far as French Polynesia, Hawaii, parts of New Guinea, Tonga and the Cook Islands. Chieftains will rule these countries until Europeans arrive.

AD 1000 — New Zealand
The Maori (migrating from islands in the north) are the first people to settle New Zealand. They live in small groups ruled by chiefs.

• See page 54
MAORI TRADITIONS

1521 — Magellan
Portuguese navigator and explorer Ferdinand Magellan finds a route to the Pacific by sailing round the southern tip of America. He reaches Guam Island.

1565 — Guam
The island of Guam is claimed as a territory by Spain.

1642-1643 — Tasman
Dutch navigator and explorer Abel Tasman, working for the *Dutch East India Company*, discovers Tasmania, New Zealand, Tonga and Fiji. He circumnavigates Australia, but does not see it.

1770 — Captain Cook
British explorer and navigator Captain James Cook, in his ship *The Endeavour*, sets out to find the much predicted *Southern continent – Terra Australis*. On 19 April, 1770, he discovers the southeast coast of Australia.

• The TIMELINE continues on page 53

OCEANIA

Oceania comprises Australia, New Zealand and around 20,000 Pacific islands, many of which are uninhabited. Oceania has the smallest population of any continent. The populations of Australia and New Zealand are a mixture of indigenous peoples and many different ethnic groups who have migrated from Europe and Asia. On the Pacific islands tourism is an important industry, but many communities maintain a traditional way of life, living in small villages, fishing, growing crops and raising livestock.

A Huli warrior from Papua New Guinea. Huli boys attend *'wig school'* for several years. They grow their hair and learn to care for it. When the hair is long enough, it is cut and made into a fantastic wig.

TOTAL POPULATION

Total population of Oceania:

32,700,000

COUNTRIES BY POPULATION

Oceania countries with highest population:

Australia	20,090,437
Papua New Guinea	5,545,268
New Zealand	4,035,461

Lowest population:

Wallis and Futuna Islands	16,025
Nauru	13,048
Tuvalu	11,636

POPULATION GROWTH

Population growth rates per year in Oceania:

Australia	0.87%
Fiji	1.4%
New Zealand	1.02%
Papua New Guinea	2.26%
Solomon Islands	2.68%

STATISTICS: PEOPLE OF OCEANIA

Average life expectancy across continent:

Male:	68.5 years
Female:	74 years

Highest life expectancy:

Australia	80 years

Lowest life expectancy:

Kiribati	62 years

Death rate: 6
(average annual number of deaths per 1000 people)

Birth rate: 22
(average annual number of births per 1000 people)

Total fertility rate: 3
(average number of children born per woman)

Infant mortality:
20 deaths per 1000 live births
(number of deaths of infants under one year old per year):

AGE STRUCTURE

MEDIAN AGE is the age that divides a population in two – half the people are younger than this age and half are older.

Median age for Oceania

Total population:	25 years
Male:	25 years
Female:	25 years

Age structure
The charts (right) show the age structure of the populations of three Oceanian countries.

Australia
13% 19.8% 67.2%

Marshall Islands
2.7% 38.2% 59.1%

French Polynesia
5.9% 26.7% 67.4%

Key

0-14
15-64
65+

MAP OF OCEANIA

NORTH PACIFIC OCEAN

NORTHERN MARIANA ISLANDS
Guam
Marianas Trench

MICRONESIA

MELANESIA

HAWAIIAN ISLANDS (U.S.)

MARSHALL ISLANDS

PALAU

KIRIBATI

INDONESIA

PAPUA NEW GUINEA

NAURU

SOLOMON ISLANDS

Tokelau

VANUATU

TUVALU

American Samoa

French Polynesia

FIJI

TONGA

Tahiti

New Caledonia

WALLIS AND FUTUNA ISLANDS

Cook Islands

Norfolk Islands

Great Barrier Reef

Coral Sea

AUSTRALIA

POLYNESIA

South West Pacific Basin

SOUTH PACIFIC OCEAN

INDIAN OCEAN

Tasman Sea

NEW ZEALAND

• See page 54 FARMING IN THE AUSTRALIAN OUTBACK

A farmer, in New South Wales, Australia, drives his sheep using a small truck. The southwest of Australia has grasslands and eucalyptus forests where huge flocks of sheep are raised.

ANNUAL INCOME (PER PERSON)

This chart gives an overview of the average annual income per person in 10 Oceanian countries. It ranges from the highest income to the lowest.

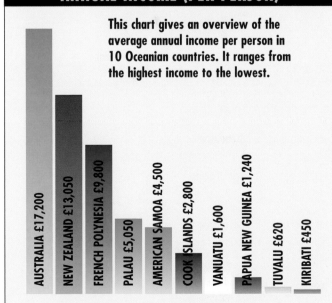

AUSTRALIA £17,200
NEW ZEALAND £13,050
FRENCH POLYNESIA £9,800
PALAU £5,050
AMERICAN SAMOA £4,500
COOK ISLANDS £2,800
VANUATU £1,600
PAPUA NEW GUINEA £1,240
TUVALU £620
KIRIBATI £450

POPULATION BELOW POVERTY LINE

Papua New Guinea	37%
Micronesia (Federated states of)	26.7%
Fiji	25.5%

• See GLOSSARY for a definition of POVERTY LINE.

INTERNET USERS

COUNTRY	INTERNET USERS
Australia	9,472,000
New Zealand	2,110,000
Papua New Guinea	75,000
Fiji	55,000
Guam	50,000
French Polynesia	35,000

• This list represents the Oceanian countries with the highest number of Internet users.

OCEANIA TIMELINE

1788 — Australia colonised
The British land at Sydney Cove and colonise Australia. Britain uses its new colony as a place to take criminals. The settlers disregard the indigenous aborigines, seizing land and destroying many sacred Aboriginal places.

• See page 54 ABORIGINES AND DREAMTIME

Early 1800s — Missionaries
Christian Missionaries travel to many parts of Oceania, especially the Polynesian islands.

1842 — French Polynesia
Polynesian territories become French Polynesia under French rule.

1898 — Guam to USA
Spain gives over Guam Island to the USA after 400 years of rule. Guam will become a US military base in the 1940s.

1899 — Samoa
Germany and the USA divide the Samoan Archipelago between them into Eastern (American) Samoa and Western Samoa.

1901 — Australia
The six British colonies in Australia become the *Commonwealth of Australia* – an independent country, but with the British monarch as formal head of state.

1904 — Western Samoa
New Zealand occupies German-ruled Western Samoa in 1914 and controls the country until it gains independence in 1962 and becomes Samoa.

1939 - 1945 World War II
Many Oceanian countries are involved in WWII. Australia, New Zealand and others fight against Japan and Germany.

1967 — Right to vote
Australia's population vote "Yes" in a referendum to finally give Aboriginal people a vote and citizenship rights in their own country.

2000 — Millennium Olympics
Sydney, Australia, hosts the Millennium Olympics.

PEOPLE *of* OCEANIA

MAORI TRADITIONS

The Maori people were the first settlers in New Zealand. They arrived from Polynesia around 1000 years ago.

Today the Maori number over 300,000 and *Maoritanga*, the Maori language, is used by many people.

Many ancient traditions are still maintained, such as *ta moko*, Maori tattooing. Many Maori men tattoo their faces and their bodies.

The traditional *haka* dance can also be seen. It was originally performed at the onset of war to unite the people.

Culture fact: *Maoris greet each other using the bongi – a traditional nose-to-nose touch.*

Leg, arm, foot, hand and even tongue movements are all important in the haka.

VANUATU – THE PENTECOST JUMP

Pentecost is one of the 80 islands which make up the republic of Vanuatu.

In spring, the Pentecost islanders use vines and branches to build a 30-metre-high tower.

The island's boys and men attach vines to their feet and hurl themselves from the tower. The jumpers aim for their vine to tighten, stopping their fall, as near to the ground as possible.

It is believed that this dangerous ritual will make the ground fertile and the crops grow. But jumpers are often killed!

Culture fact: *the Pentecost jump has inspired the modern craze of bungee-jumping.*

It takes the islanders around five weeks to build the tower.

ABORIGINES AND DREAMTIME

Although all native Australians are known as Aborigines, there are many different groups. Aboriginal people have lived in every part of Australia for around 60,000 years.

Aborigines live in extended family groups, and the whole community help to raise the children. Elders are highly respected because they are the bridge between the past and the present.

Aboriginal knowledge and practices are linked to *Dreamtime*, the stories of creation. Ancestral spirits came to Earth and taught the people how to live and how to respect the animals and plants that had been created.

Across Australia there are Dreamtime tracks, paths taken by the spirits as they created the land.

Today, some Aborigines live in cities, but other communities still maintain a traditional, rural life, living and hunting in *'the bush'*. Aborigines only take from the land the animals and plants they need for food.

Culture fact: *before they can become men, young Aboriginal boys make a journey, all alone, into the wilderness to prove they can survive. This is known as a 'walkabout'.*

• *See page 10 HOLY PLACES AROUND THE WORLD.*

Traditional styles of painting depict the Aboriginal Dreamtime stories.

FARMING IN THE AUSTRALIAN OUTBACK

In the vast outback area between the coasts and desert of Australia, are thousands of outback farms known as *'stations'*.

Just one farm can cover around 3000 square kilometres of land.

The sheep and cattle graze over huge areas and farmers use quadbikes, motorbikes and even helicopters when they need to round up their animals.

Outback farmers have to cope with some of the hottest and driest conditions in the world. In times of drought, trucks take food and water out to sheep and cattle.

Lifestyle fact: *children living on outback farms can be educated through the Internet, and by lessons over the radio – called 'The School of the Air'.*

OCEANIA FACTFILES

Oceania

Each factfile contains: **life expectancy** and **infant mortality** figures (important indicators of quality of life and general health); **ethnic groups** and **religions** (shown as a percentage of the population, where figures are available); **main languages spoken** (listed in order of number of speakers); **literacy rates** (where available); and the **top five industries** ranked by the amount of money they produce for the country each year.

AMERICAN SAMOA

Total population: 57,881
Life expectancy: 75 years
Infant mortality: 9 deaths
Ethnic mix: Native Pacific islander 92.9%; Asian 2.9%; others 4.2%
Religions: Christianity
Languages: Samoan; English
Literacy rate – male: 98% / female: 97%
Industries: Tuna canneries; handicrafts

AUSTRALIA

Total population: 20,090,437
Life expectancy: 80 years
Infant mortality: 5 deaths
Ethnic mix: White 92%; Asian 7%; Aboriginal and others 1%
Religions: Christian 67.4%; others 32.6%
Languages: English
Literacy rate – male: 100% / female: 100%
Industries (top 5): Mining; industrial and transport equipment; food processing; chemicals; steel

COOK ISLANDS
Total population: 21,388
(No life expectancy or infant mortality statistics available)
Ethnic mix: Maori 87.7%; others 12.3%   Religions: Christianity
Languages: English; Maori
Literacy rate – male: 95% / female: 95%
Industries (top 5): Fruit; tourism; fishing; clothing; handicrafts

FIJI

Total population: 893,354
Life expectancy: 69.5 years
Infant mortality: 13 deaths
Ethnic mix: Fijian 51%; Indian 44%; others 5%
Religions: Christian 52%; Hindu 38%; Muslim 8%; others 2%
Languages: English; Fijian; Hindustani
Literacy rate – male: 95.5% / female: 91.9%
Industries (top 5): Tourism; sugar; clothing; copra; gold and silver

FRENCH POLYNESIA
Total population: 270,485
Life expectancy: 76 years
Infant mortality: 8 deaths
Ethnic mix: Polynesian 78%; Chinese 12%; French 10%
Religions: Protestant 54%; Roman Catholic 30%; others 16%
Languages: French; Polynesian
Literacy rate (total population): 98%
Industries (top 5): Tourism; pearls; agriculture; handicrafts; phosphates

GUAM
Total population: 168,564
Life expectancy: 78 years
Infant mortality: 7 deaths
Ethnic mix: Chamorro 37.1%; Filipino 26.3%; other Pacific islanders 11.3%; white 6.9%; others 18.4%
Religions: Roman Catholic 85%; others 15%
Languages: English; Chamorro; Philippine languages
Literacy rate – male: 99% / female: 99%
Industries (top 5): US military-related industry; tourism; construction; shipping services; concrete products

KIRIBATI
Total population: 103,092
Life expectancy: 62 years
Infant mortality: 48.5 deaths
Ethnic mix: Micronesian 98.8%; others 1.2%
Religions: Roman Catholic 52%; Protestant 40%; others 8%
Languages: I-Kiribati; English
Industries: Fishing; handicrafts

MARSHALL ISLANDS

Total population: 59,071
Life expectancy: 70 years
Infant mortality: 29 deaths
Ethnic mix: Micronesian
Religions: Protestant 54.8%; Assembly of God 25.8%; others 19.4%
Languages: Marshallese; English
Literacy rate – male: 93.6% / female: 93.7%
Industries: Copra; tuna processing; tourism; shell, wood and pearl crafts

MICRONESIA (FEDERATED STATES OF)

Total population: 108,105
Life expectancy: 70 years
Infant mortality: 30 deaths
Ethnic mix: Nine different ethnic Micronesian and Polynesian groups
Religions: Roman Catholic 50%; Protestant 47%; others 3%
Languages: English; Trukese; Pohnpeian; Yapese; Kosrean; Ulithian
Literacy rate – male: 91% / female: 88%
Industries (top 5): Tourism; construction; fish processing; aquaculture; craft items from shell, wood and pearls

NAURU

Total population: 13,048
Life expectancy: 63 years
Infant mortality: 10 deaths
Ethnic mix: Nauruan 58%; other Pacific islanders 26%; others 16%
Religions: Christianity
Languages: Nauruan; English
Industries: Phosphate mining; offshore banking; coconut products

NEW CALEDONIA
Total population: 216,494
Life expectancy: 74 years
Infant mortality: 8 deaths
Ethnic mix: Melanesian 42.5%; European 37.1%; others 20.4%
Religions: Roman Catholic 60%; Protestant 30%; others 10%
Languages: French; 33 Melanesian/Polynesian dialects
Literacy rate – male: 92% / female: 90%
Industries: Nickel mining and smelting

NEW ZEALAND

Total population: 4,035,461
Life expectancy: 79 years
Infant mortality: 6 deaths
Ethnic mix: European 69.8%; Maori 7.9%; Asian 5.7%; others 16.6%
Religions: Christianity
Languages: English; Maori
Literacy rate (total population): 99%
Industries (top 5): Food processing; wood and paper products; textiles; machinery and transport equipment; banking and insurance

NORTHERN MARIANA ISLANDS

Total population: 80,362
Life expectancy: 76 years
Infant mortality: 7 deaths
Ethnic mix: Asian 56.3%; Pacific islander 36.3%; others 7.4%
Religions: Christianity
Languages: Philippine languages; Chinese; Chamorro; English
Literacy rate (total population): 97%
Industries: Tourism; construction; clothing; handicrafts

PALAU

Total population: 20,303
Life expectancy: 70 years
Infant mortality: 15 deaths
Ethnic mix: Palauan (Micronesian with Malayan and Melanesian)
Religions: Roman Catholic 94%; Protestant 6%
Languages: Palauan; English; Tobi; Angaur
Literacy rate – male: 93% / female: 90%
Industries: Tourism; shell, wood and pearl crafts; construction; clothing

PAPUA NEW GUINEA
Total population: 5,545,268
Life expectancy: 65 years
Infant mortality: 51 deaths
Ethnic mix: Melanesian; Papuan; Negrito; Micronesian; Polynesian
Religions: Indigenous beliefs 34%; Roman Catholic 22%; others 44%
Languages: Melanesian; over 800 indigenous languages
Literacy rate – male: 71.1% / female: 57.7%
Industries (top 5): Copra crushing; palm oil processing; plywood production; wood chip production; mining (gold, silver and copper)

SAMOA

Total population: 177,287
Life expectancy: 71 years
Infant mortality: 28 deaths   Ethnic mix: Samoan 92.6%; Euronesians (European/Polynesian) 7.4%
Religions: Christian 82.1%; others 17.9%
Languages: Samoan; English
Literacy rate (total population): 99.7%
Industries: Food processing; construction materials; car parts

SOLOMON ISLANDS

Total population: 538,032
Life expectancy: 73 years
Infant mortality: 21 deaths
Ethnic mix: Melanesian 94.5%; Polynesian 3%; others 2.5%
Religions: Church of Melanesia 32.8%; Roman Catholic 19%; South Seas Evangelical 17%; others 31.2%
Languages: Melanesian; English; 120 indigenous languages
Industries: Fishing (tuna); mining; timber

TONGA

Total population: 112,422
Life expectancy: 70 years
Infant mortality: 13 deaths
Ethnic mix: Polynesian
Religions: Christianity   Languages: Tongan; English
Literacy rate – male: 98.4% / female: 98.7%
Industries: Tourism; fishing

TUVALU

Total population: 11,636
Life expectancy: 68 years
Infant mortality: 20 deaths
Ethnic mix: Polynesian 96%; Micronesian 4%
Religions: Church of Tuvalu (Congregationalist) 97%; others 3%
Languages: Tuvaluan; English; Samoan; Kiribati (on island of Nui)
Industries: Fishing; tourism; copra

VANUATU
Total population: 205,754
Life expectancy: 62.5 years
Infant mortality: 55 deaths
Ethnic mix: Melanesian 98%; others 2%
Religions: Christian 76.7%; indigenous beliefs 7.6%; others 15.7%
Languages: English; French; 100 indigenous languages
Literacy rate – male: 57% / female: 48%
Industries: Food and fish freezing; wood processing; meat canning

WALLIS AND FUTUNA ISLANDS
Total population: 16,025
(No life expectancy or infant mortality statistics available)
Ethnic mix: Polynesian   Religions: Roman Catholic
Languages: Wallisian; Futunian; French
Literacy rate – male: 50% / female: 50%
Industries: Copra; handicrafts; fishing; timber

• See THE GLOSSARY for terms used in these FACTFILES.

BASIC NEEDS

In order to survive all people need:

- *Water*
- *Food*
- *Shelter*
- *Sanitation*
- *Health care*

To live full, dignified lives they need:

- *Education*
- *Work*
- *Freedom, security and justice*
- *A say in their future*

HUMAN RIGHTS

The United Nations' 1948 Universal Declaration of Human Rights lists the rights which all member states should respect. They include:

- *equality between the sexes and races*
- *the right to a fair trial*
- *the right to vote and to join political parties and trade unions*
- *freedom from torture or cruel punishment*
- *freedom of religious belief*
- *asylum from persecution*
- *the right to social security*
- *the right to work*
- *the right to an adequate standard of living*
- *the right to education*

The people of the world live in a wide variety of different ways. But all people have some things in common: they have the same basic needs, should have the same rights, and face many of the same problems. To provide these needs, respect these rights, and solve these problems, is the challenge of the 21st century. It is a challenge for the people suffering the problems, and for the world's leaders.

Malnourished young children in Sudan in Africa. Many children in the world have been hungry their whole lives.

WATER FACTS

An average adult in the USA or UK uses around 540 litres of water each day.

Everybody needs at least 23 litres of water each day, and it must be clean because dirty water can cause disease and death. People also need proper sanitation (safe, clean ways to deal with human waste).

However:

- More than one billion people in the poor countries of the world do not have clean water.
- Over 2 billion people do not have proper sanitation.
- There are increasing water shortages even in rich countries.

HEALTH FACTS

Millions of people suffer and die from preventable illnesses in the poor countries of the world. The most serious disease of all is HIV/AIDs. There are drugs which can treat HIV, but they are too expensive for poor people in poor countries.

At the end of 2004:

- 39.5 million people were living with HIV/AIDs.
- There were 15 million AIDs orphans: children who had lost one or both parents to AIDs. This figure is expected to rise to 44 million by 2010.

More than 12 million children in Africa have been orphaned by AIDs. In South Africa the average age that someone dies of AIDs is 37.

ENVIRONMENT FACTS

People are damaging the environment in many ways, but the biggest environmental threat is climate change.

When we burn coal, oil and gas we create greenhouse gases which warm up the Earth. Scientists predict that within this century, global warming will cause:

- Sea levels to rise by up to a metre – a disaster to low-lying countries such as Bangladesh.
- Drier weather in the tropics (the area around the Equator), which could cause more famines in Africa.
- Extreme weather such as storms and floods.

Environmental campaigners worry that world leaders aren't doing enough to prevent global warming.

- *Compare the LIFE EXPECTANCY and INFANT MORTALITY RATE statistics in the FACTFILES of countries in AFRICA and ASIA with those in EUROPE and NORTH AMERICA to see the effect of living in poverty, with poor sanitation and limited healthcare.*

WAR AND REFUGEE FACTS

War facts

There are ongoing conflicts in many of the world's countries, including:

- Afghanistan
- Colombia
- Iraq
- Israel, the Gaza Strip and the West Bank
- Sudan
- Uganda

- 90% of casualties in modern wars are civilians.

- Billions of pounds are spent by governments around the world on wars each year. This money could be used to improve people's lives.

Refugee facts

- Refugees are people who have fled from war and persecution.

- At the beginning of 2005, there were 19.2 million refugees around the world.

NUMBER OF REFUGEES WORLDWIDE

North America 853,300

Europe 4,429,900

Asia 6,899,600

South & Central America 2,070,800

Africa 4,861,400

Oceania 82,400

EDUCATION FACTS

Education is the key to escaping poverty, but many poor countries cannot afford to provide free education for all of their children.

Around the world today:

- 23% of people aged 15 or over cannot read or write.

- Girls are less likely to go to school than boys.

- 186 million children aged between 5 and 14 have to work for a living to help support their families, and do not get the chance to go to school.

These school children in Calcutta, India, are holding a placard to promote children's rights during a rally highlighting the issue of child labour. India has the largest number of child workers of any country in the world, around 80 million children.

POVERTY FACTS

Most of the world's poor people live in South America, Africa, and Asia. In poor countries around the world:

- 1.2 billion people live on less than one dollar a day.

- 800 million people are malnourished.

- 30,000 children die every day because they are poor.

The leaders of the world's richest countries, meeting in July 2005, agreed to give more help to poor countries, by:

- Increasing aid to $50 billion a year by 2010.

- Cancelling the debts of 18 poor countries.

Many people think that rich countries could and should do a lot more, especially to make trade between rich and poor countries more fair.

THE FUTURE

The world's population has grown fast in the past 200 years, and especially in the last 50 years.

The rate of population growth is beginning to slow down, but the big question is whether the world's population will stabilise at 8, 10, or 12 billion — and when? All these people will need somewhere to live, food to eat and water to drink.

GLOSSARY

AD In the Christian calendar this indicates events which took place after the birth of Christ and stands for *Anno Domini: in the year of our Lord.* See also BC; BCE; CE

Afrikaans An official language of South Africa, closely related to Dutch.

agro-industries The manufacture of agricultural equipment and machinery.

American Indian reservations Land reserved for a native American Indian tribe to move into when it gave up to the white government the land on which it had formerly lived.

Americo-Liberians Liberia is an independent state in west Africa founded by the *American Colonization Society* in 1822 as a home for freed American slaves. Americo-Liberians are the descendants of those immigrants.

Amerindian A word used to describe Native Americans, or American Indians. When Christopher Columbus reached the New World he thought he had reached Asia and the East Indies, which is why the word Indian first came to be used in connection with people living in America.

Animal of the Year
The Chinese Lunar Calendar has a cycle of twelve years. Each of the twelve years is named after an animal: Rat, Ox, Tiger, Rabbit, Dragon, Snake Horse, Sheep, Monkey, Rooster, Dog and Boar.

Animist An animist believes that all natural objects, including stones and metals, are inhabited by a soul or supernatural being.

Arawaks The name given to the friendly native people whom the Spanish first met when they came to the Caribbean.

Aryan tribes A group of tribes of fair and blue-eyed northern people who spoke Sanskrit. They moved into northern India and merged with the local population. Other Aryan groups spread further west into Europe, and eventually as far as Ireland.

Ash Wednesday In the Christian calendar Ash Wednesday is the first day of Lent (the six-week period before Easter). It is a time of fasting, sorrow for sin, and for thinking about death. As a sign of sorrow it was traditional to wear sackcloth, and to cover one's head with ashes.

Bantu Refers to over 400 different ethnic groups in Africa (from Cameroon to South Africa). Bantu people are united by a common *'language family'*, and in many cases, customs.

Basques A people of unknown origin mainly living around the western Pyrenees in France and Spain. Their language has no known relationship with any other language.

bauxite The ore from which aluminium is extracted.

BC In the Christian calendar this indicates events which took place before the birth of Christ: *Before Christ.* See also AD; BCE; CE

BCE In the modern calendar this is a recently introduced replacement for BC (see above) as a more inclusive term and stands for *Before the Common Era.* See also AD; CE

Berbers A people belonging to northwest Africa, chiefly living in Morocco and Algeria, although some now live in Egypt and as far south as Burkina Faso.

Bretons A Celtic people with their own language, largely living in Brittany, France.

bush An uncultivated or sparsely settled area, especially in Africa, Australia, New Zealand or Canada.

calcium carbide A grey salt of calcium used in the production of the flammable gas acetylene.

Caribs The second group of native people (after the Arawaks, see above) met by Columbus.

CE In the modern calendar this is a recently introduced replacement for AD (see above) as a more inclusive term and stands for *Common Era.* See also BC; BCE

Civil War A war between two groups of people within the same country.

Colonies Countries which have been taken over by another country, and are governed by that country. It can also refer to a group of people who have chosen to settle in another country, but have maintained links with their mother country.

copra The oil-yielding kernel of the coconut.

Creole A person born in Central or South America of European ancestry, or of mixed European and black ancestry. A Creole language has features of both languages from which it is derived: the local language and a European language.

Cultures The total range of activities and ideas of a group of people with shared traditions.

Eightfold Path The Buddha's teaching was set out in the *Four Noble Truths*, the fourth of which is the *Noble Eightfold Path*, showing the way to end suffering. It comprises Right knowledge; Right attitude; Right speech; Right action; Right living; Right effort; Right mindfulness; Right composure. The eight items of the path may be classified under three headings: the first two: wisdom or understanding; the next three: ethical conduct; the last three: mental discipline.

Ethnic groups Groups of people who share common racial, linguistic or religious features.

Evangelical Lutheran
A Protestant Christian church placing great emphasis on the teaching of the Bible. It is named after Martin Luther who was the first to protest against aspects of the Roman Catholic church in the sixteenth century.

Five Pillars of Islam The five duties Muslims have to observe. They are: recitation of the creed; ritual prayer; almsgiving; fasting during the month of Ramadan, and the Hajj (see below).

Four noble truths The expression of the Buddha's experience: *1) The universal human experience of suffering, mental, emotional and physical, is the effect of past evil (karma). 2) The cause of suffering is craving the wrong things, or the right things in the wrong way. 3) It is possible for suffering to cease. 4) The solution is the Eightfold Path (see above).*

Fulani A people who live in West Africa and are primarily nomadic herders and traders, with numerous established trade routes. They originally came from North Africa and the Middle East, and are known as 'white people' to many Africans because they have lighter skin and straighter hair. They were the first people in West Africa to convert to Islam.

Gaelic Any of the closely related Celtic languages of the Celts in Ireland, Scotland or the Isle of Man.

Geisha A professional female companion for men in Japan. Geishas are trained in music, dance, and the art of conversation.

geothermal power The power generated using steam produced by the heat coming from the molten core of the Earth.

gypsum A colourless or white mineral. It is used in the manufacture of plaster of Paris, cement, paint, school chalk, glass and fertilizer.

Hajj The pilgrimage to Mecca which is one of the *Five Pillars of Islam* (see above), and which Muslims are obliged to make at least once in a lifetime. In Mecca, pilgrims make seven circuits of the *Kaaba* and touch the *Black Stone*.

Hausa A member of a black people of west Africa living chiefly in northern Nigeria.

Hispanic A term used in the USA for immigrants who come from the Spanish-speaking countries of Central America.

Hutu The largest of the three ethnic groups in Burundi and Rwanda. They probably arrived in the area in the 1st century, displacing the Twa. They dominated the area until the 15th century when they were conquered by the Tutsi.

Igbo A black people living in south-eastern Nigeria.

Immigrants see Migrants

Indigenous Originating or occurring naturally within a country or a region. It can refer to people or plants or animals. Another word is 'native' which has the root meaning of being born in a place.

Industrial Revolution The introduction of steam power in the manufacture of textiles and other goods during the late 18th and early 19th centuries.

It began in England, and led to many workers who had worked from home in the countryside moving to towns to work in the new factories.

Life expectancy The average number of years a person can be expected to live in a particular country or place. It is a measure of the quality of life in a country, including health and wealth.

Malnutrition The lack of food, or the proper kinds of food to maintain health.

Mestizo A word derived from the Portuguese word for 'mixed'. It is the name given to people of mixed European and Amerindian descent throughout the Americas.

Migrants People who move from the place where they were born to settle in another place. Emigrants are the people moving out of a country. Immigrants are people moving into a country.

Mormon A member of the *Church of Jesus Christ of Latter Day Saints* founded in 1830 in

the USA by Joseph Smith. The church's followers later moved to Salt Lake City, USA, under their leader Brigham Young.

Mulatto A person having one black and one white parent.

Orthodox The Christian churches which broke away from the Roman Catholic church at the 'schism' in 1054. They are chiefly found in Greece, Russia and the Balkan countries.

Pagan A religion which believes in many gods.

Papiamento A Spanish Creole language which is mixed with Dutch, Portuguese and English.

Pashtuns A Muslim people of eastern Iranian origin, living mainly in Afghanistan and Pakistan.

Patois A simplified spoken form of a language, often French or English, which has been adapted by people in a particular region.

Pilgrim Fathers The English Puritans who sailed in the *Mayflower* to New England (USA) and founded the Plymouth Colony in Massachusetts in 1620.

Pilgrimage A journey to a sacred place, or for a special reason. See also Hajj; Pilgrim Fathers.

Poverty line The level of income below which a person cannot afford to buy all the resources they need to live.

Pygmies Peoples of short stature in Central Africa.

Santeria A religion started in Cuba by the slaves brought from West Africa. It is a combination of their traditional African religion and Spanish Catholicism.

Shona An agricultural people linguistically related to the Bantu.

Tajiks The original Iranian population of Afghanistan and Turkistan (now Turkmenistan, Kazakhstan, Uzbekistan, Tajikistan, Kyrgystan and part of China). They are settled grain and fruit farmers. Their crafts were highly developed and their towns along the routes linking Persia, China and India were centres of trade.

Tamils A people from South Asia mainly in southern India and north-east Sri Lanka.

Tatars A Turkic people who moved west with the Mongols in the 7th century and settled in eastern Europe, including the Crimean peninsula (now part of Ukraine).

Tickertape parades Tickertape is the continuous ribbon of paper produced by a machine automatically printing current stock quotations. A tickertape parade is the showering of these ribbons of paper from the windows of offices onto a parade in the street below.

Trick or Treat A Halloween tradition, originating in the USA. Children knock on doors asking people for a *'treat'* (such as sweets), or threatening a *'trick'* – doing something unpleasant!

Tutsi One of the three ethnic groups living in Rwanda and Burundi.

Twa A pygmy people, of short stature, and the oldest recorded inhabitants of the area in central Africa now comprising Rwanda, Burundi and the Democratic Republic of Congo.

Uzbeks Originally a nomadic people from a Mongolian ethnic group. They are primarily Muslim.

Voodoo A religious cult of West African origin, but largely practised in Haiti. It involves witchcraft. Followers are believed to be able to communicate with ancestors and animistic deities while in a trance.

Wolof A member of a black people of west Africa living mainly in Senegal.

Xhosa A member of a cattle-rearing black people of southern Africa, living mainly in the Cape Province of South Africa.

Yoruba A member of a black people of west Africa living

chiefly in the coastal regions of south west Nigeria. They are skilled sculptors, working in wood and brass and occasionally terracotta. Yoruba is also an African language.

Zionist (in Swaziland) A blend of Christianity and indigenous ancestral worship. The word was also used for a supporter of the movement to re-establish a Jewish homeland in Palestine.

INDEX

The letters a, b, c, d following the page number indicate the column (lettering from left to right) in which the information may be found on that page.